Dear Parents

A Collection of Letters to Bereaved Parents

Edited by Joy Johnson
Illustration and Design by New Idea Design
A Centering Corporation Resource

Copyright ©1989
Revised 1998
Centering Corporation

ISBN: 1-56123-033-2
San: 298-1815

ADDITIONAL COPIES MAY BE ORDERED FROM:
Centering Corporation
1531 N Saddle Creek Rd Omaha, NE 68104
Phone: 402-553-1200 Fax: 402-553-0507
Email: J1200@aol.com

Sharing Letters from:

Illness:

Sudden Death

Infant Death

Brothers and Sister

Caring Others

It is a hole,
A vacantness.
A scary hollow shell that I find myself in.
Death. The robber. The thief of certainty. The stealer of dreams.
My mind holds a thousand facts, yet there is no answer.
My child died, and, in many ways, so have I.
The Me I knew has vanished and in its place stands
a hollow mold that must be re-filled.

SANDY PRIEBE

DEAR
PARENTS

~

A
Collection
of Letters
to
Bereaved
Parents

~

4

This is a book of sharing . . .

of thoughts, ideas, feelings, advice and care. It is a book of letters to bereaved parents, from bereaved parents and nationally-known educators, authors and public leaders.

This is a book of fellowship and sharing of pain, of common feelings and expression. We asked each writer to imagine you as their guest for a cup of coffee. Because of that idea, the letters are casual and caring. They are powerful in their messages and will recognize the pain you feel. We started each with, "Dear Parents" to recognize the great number of grieving parents throughout the world.

The death of a child is probably the worst thing that can happen to a person. As Candy Lightner, founder of Mothers against Drunk Driving says in her letter:

"All the letters you will read are from those who have suffered your pain and survived. It was not easy. I still miss Cari, and sometimes I think she is the lucky one."

Illness: Then Death

Do I cry?

Of course, and who cares?

Preserve us from the persons who try to say that parents

who express violent emotions are somehow tetched.

I'd have a lot of cold nights married to anyone

with that attitude.

GRACE POWERS MONACO

Dear Parents,

I feel confused when I look at others. Parents who are bothered by a 4-year-old's halt in front of a gumball machine. I slip a penny in. A small hand turns the knob. A round red ball rolls out and is snatched up with childish purpose. Summer sandals smack along to catch up. I want to stop the mother. It is only a penny. It is only time. I want to yell. 'Wait! Don't ignore the chance for a memory!'

DEAR
PARENTS
~
A
Collection
of Letters
to
Bereaved
Parents
~
6

I seem to see things others don't see . . . opportunities for love and laughter. It's like death has removed my clouded vision. Richness is the feel of worn fur from a beloved stuffed animal cradled by a sleeping child. The finest fur money can buy will never cloak me in such comfort.

I am confused by some old friendships. There are phone numbers I dial. Messages that are never returned. A knock comes at the door. It is someone I barely know. "I just wanted you to know I always enjoyed talking with your little girl. I want you to know how sorry I am. The coffee pot is always on."

I sit and listen to lunch conversations at work. The debate about investments for retirement years. The certain talk of things 10 years down the road. I sip my coffee in silence. Their earth has not quaked yet.
Life can change in the twinkling of an eye.
Death has changed me.
It has taught me I can never count on tomorrows again.

I weary of hearing how brave I am. I weary of people saying, "I don't think I could go through what you've been through." I'm no stronger or weaker than they are. We all do what we have to do when we don't have any choice. Sure, I act normal. Sure, I smile and crack a joke. That's not brave . . . that's survival. They don't see me at night.

Sometimes when I learn of another child who is seriously ill or has died, I pound the wall. Sometimes I sit on the church steps across from my house. I read the cornerstone. 1878. I think of the weddings, the baptisms, the funerals. I think of the diseases that raged when the calloused hands fashioned this house of faith. I trace my finger tips in the mortared brick. Typhoid, diphtheria, whooping cough. Those battles are won. It's been years since my religious training, yet the story that floods my mind is the woman at the well.

I am different today than days before. I will continue to change throughout whatever tomorrows are placed in my hands. I will never return to 'normal.' I can only evolve. The empty vessel is slowly being refilled.

Sandy

DR. NORMAN HAGLEY IS THE AUTHOR OF COMFORT US, LORD.
HE WAS ALSO THE FOUNDER OF ONE OF THE EARLIEST PARENT SUPPORT GROUPS.

Dear Parents,

I suppose the simplest thing in the world for me to do is to give you a bunch of mumbo jumbo about the reasons for the death of your child. Somehow we feel we must give people reasons for everything that happens in life. There are occasions when there are no answers, and I suspect this is one of those times. All I can say to you is that what happened to you is a tragedy, a stark, human tragedy of the most monumental proportion; it is nothing more, it is nothing less.

You will have many people who will tell you such a thing is an act of God, but I want to tell you I cannot believe that is right. I do not think God has taken your child. The God I know is not in the business of destroying or killing. His task has always been to create and preserve. Those who tell you God took your child or that He needed your child for an angel in Heaven, are doing you and God a great disservice. Why would God need to cause you grief in order to create another angel? Could He have not just created another angel if He needed one more? No those, who tell you it is in the will of God are mistaken. God did not cause your child's death in order to have the child near Him. The God I know is not so limited; He can be near you and your child every day you are on this earth.

The awful truth is there may not be any recognizable or definable reason for this death. Each and every one of us is subject to the laws of nature because we have been given freedom by our creator. Now freedom brings with it certain risks. One of those risks is that we have to live in this world as it is. Consequently, we face all the good and all the evil that exist here. One of the evils is that our bodies can be attacked by disease, we can suffer accidents and we can suffer at the hands of other humans. The price for perfect freedom is high and there are times when it seems too high; but could we humans be created in the image of God if we did not have this freedom?

I do not know the reason for the death of a child, for it is not the natural order of things. It should be the parents who die, then the child. In your case the natural order has been reversed and your suffering is very real and there are no words that can take it away. All I or anyone else can do is tell you how very sorry I am and to pledge to you my understanding and unending support.

I honestly believe that God is a preserving God, a saving God. As such, He has reached out to receive the spirit of your child and drawn it close to him. In his most creative act, He has created a new life out of death.

Norman

GRACE ANN MONACO, JD, IS THE BOARD CHAIRWOMAN OF CANDLELIGHTERS
CHILDHOOD CANCER FOUNDATION, THE NETWORKING ARM OF OVER 250 GROUPS
FOR PARENTS WHOSE CHILDREN HAVE CANCER.

DEAR
PARENTS

~

A
Collection
of Letters
to
Bereaved
Parents

~

8

Dear Parents,

Kathleen Rea was 18 months when she was diagnosed in 1968 with acute lympho-cytic leukemia. She was all laughing dark eyes and chubby cheeks and swirling ringlets. She never ever looked sick (just chubbier from the medication). Even when she lost her hair, she lost it in a humorous way--she had a long forelock from the front of her head down to the middle of her back and no hair on either side; an original Mohawk.

We had two beautiful years while she was being treated for cancer. If she had been diagnosed just a little bit later, science would have caught up with her and she would have been cured. When she was diagnosed, only 20% of children with her form of cancer were saved; today, 80% are.

Kathleen Rea is sitting right across the table from me. Well, not really since she has been gone these 18 years, but I always feel as if she is beside me in spirit; teasing, criticizing, urging me on over the next hill. Our family has a deep religious faith and when Kathleen Rea left us, our priest in his eulogy said that we had not lost a daughter, we had gained an advocate in Heaven.

Kathleen Rea was ready to go, even if we weren't ready to give her up. There was no fear of what comes next; no rancor about her lot. One afternoon in the hospital she looked me straight in the eye and asked if she was going to be able to come home. I asked her what she thought and she replied that she thought her machinery was all worn out and they couldn't fix it. I asked her what she thought would hap-pen if she didn't come home. Kathleen Rea said that she would go to heaven and keep her great-grandfather Fitz-Gibbons company. She had never met him, but we told stories about him and she said she would drink beer and eat cheese and play cards and get to know him. (Fortunately, she left out the cigars.)

What am I trying to tell you? If your child is ready to go; reluctant, but ready, you have to be ready to let them feel comfortable about going and let them know they are not letting you down. One thing I have learned in my 18-year association with Candlelighters is that our kids worry a lot about how their illness affects us; whether we are strong enough to take it. They need reassurance.

Candlelighters was only a few months into beginning its programs when Kathleen Rea died. I found wonderful friends. I gave them all cauliflower ear from talking about my feelings on the phone. But Candlelighters gave me something else. It gave me a whole other second family of children to invest time and energy and caring in. My family and I all got involved right down to licking envelopes.

Whenever I write a letter counseling a family about cancer treatments, or an insurance problem or lobbying to get one of our cured sons or daughters into the armed services, I increase my vested ownership in all our cancer children. Their successes thrill me; their setbacks tug at my heartstrings. I know that what was learned in treating Kathleen Rea is saving other lives and that gives me a share of those lives. Kathleen Rea's legacy to me is my legacy of caring and sharing to them and to their families.

Do I cry? Of course, and who cares? Preserve from us the persons who try to say that parents who express violent emotions are somehow tetched. I'd have a lot of cold nights married to anyone with that attitude.

Share your emotions--particularly with peers. When Candlelighters started we learned how wonderful it was to have friends we could have a good time with; relax with, who would not look at us and say – "you pervert, how can you have a good time when your child is sick or dying?" I suppose there are some dingbats who feel the same way after you have lost a child. To get through it, to be able to be the best person/parents you can be to your spouse, your children, you need to be able to find a way to enjoy yourself, take time for yourself.

I remember meeting a mother at a conference in San Antonio who could have been a twin. We lost our daughters within months of each other. We went up to the top of the revolving restaurant, told the waiter we would be doing a lot of crying, just keep the wine carafe filled and the food coming and not to get freaked out. We talked about our children and cried a lot and it was an affectionate release; it was a cleansing relief.

When I go on speaking engagements and get taken proudly through the wards to meet the children in all stages of their cancers, I remember what Kathleen Rea went through and that night in my room I cry again and laugh a little.

When Kathleen Rea died, for 6 months, all I could remember was the bloated, blotchy, misshapen body that she was at death. By February of the next year I remembered how beautiful she was, how indomitable her spirit was, how much striving I would have to do in my own life to match her courage and determination. Five years after her death I was still crying in church when they came to prayers for the faithful departed. My priest told me to cry away; he told me that everyone understood the sadness that comes from missing the special spark and spirit that is unique to each child. I can remember the happy times now and I don't cry as much but I will mourn forever. To close off these feelings would be to amputate a part of me, a part of my life. It would be to deny that she was ever here--the pain of that would be far worse than an occasional tear.

Grace

HELEN GOODRICH LEDDY IS A GROWING, LOVING AND SEARCHING WOMAN WHO LIVES IN MAINE. HER SON, SCOTT, DIED OF CANCER WHEN HE WAS 9 YEARS OLD.

Dear Parents,

In another month, Scott will have been gone for 13 years. Sometimes, I cannot remember him at all and other times he is so real and present that I can hardly believe that so much time has passed since his death.

I have his death in perspective and I no longer weep at the thought of what we both have missed, but I am constantly amazed at how he will come to mind at the strangest moments. Much of the time, I cannot anticipate the situations which will remind me of him or the children whose behavior will cause me to reminisce.

It has not always been so. There were times when I could not bear to think about him or see other kids at play. There were times when I wanted to talk about him incessantly and other times when I didn't even want to think about what we had been through. I punished myself for things I didn't do during his illness, for things I didn't know, and during the five years that I worked with dying children and their parents, I relived my own experiences and frequently found myself lacking. Other parents seemed to have done it so much 'better' than I.

All that has passed. I have forgiven myself for the times I didn't stay at the hospital, for the questions I didn't ask and for my lack of assertiveness when it came to dealing with the medical community. I concentrate on the love we shared and the knowledge that I gave what I could to Scott and he knew, always, how much I loved and cared about him.

And--best of all--I accept my vulnerability and I know that I will forever have times when I am lonely for him, when I feel betrayed by his loss and I feel angry because he died. I know that I miss him most during family milestones, because he is not there to celebrate or be a part of an important occasion. But, it is alright to say that and to talk about him, for all of us feel the same way.

Be patient with yourselves. We all grieve in our way and time. Accept love from others and ask for what you need. Those who can give it will be there for you and those who can't or won't will fall by the wayside. You will find new friends who can share your pain and your memories. The beauty that you and your child shared together, even for a short time, will always be remembered. Do not fear that getting on with life will cause you to forget.

If there is a Parent Support group in your area, try to join. The healing that takes place as you share with others is invaluable. You are cared about by all of us who have lost a beloved child. I send you my love and peaceful thoughts.

Helen

DEAR
PARENTS

~

A
Collection
of Letters
to
Bereaved
Parents

~

10

THERESE GOODRICH IS A PAST EXECUTIVE DIRECTOR OF THE COMPASSIONATE FRIENDS IN THE UNITED STATES. TCF IS A WORLD-WIDE SUPPORT GROUP FOR BEREAVED PARENTS.

Dear Parents,

The one phrase we hear more than any other is, "It'll take time for you to get over it." We know that this is spoken with care and love. But little do we know at the beginning of our grief just what time means. The first time--the day time--the night time--the last time, all of these times.--The one thing I can say is "take it." Take all the time you need. Grief work is hard work and we need to take the time for it.

Take the time to feel . . . it's hard but worth it. We can't just push those feelings aside because they are part of who we are, how we've managed, the life we've had, all combine to affect our feelings.

Take the time to talk. Talk to anyone who seems to care about you. Ask your friends and family if they will take time to listen as you talk. If you need a tele-phone listener call the National Office of TCF, 630-990-0010, or one of the local chap-ter listeners.

Take the time to read. When you read the experiences of others, you will realize that you're not alone. Maybe a special book will help you understand what is hap-pening to you during this time we call bereavement; take the time to read and re-read the paragraphs or chapters that help.

Take the time to take care of yourself. If you like to walk, jog or run, go out and use that time to help you feel better. Get enough rest. Take the time to sleep late some days, or go to bed earlier if you need to. Sleeping may be an escape but if it helps you, take the time for an extra few hours. Take care of yourself by eating better. Try to understand what foods give you some energy and what foods help you to satisfy unmet needs. Food is always better for you than drugs or alcohol and a small weight gain or loss is not unusual. Take the time to understand what is happening to your body.

Take the time to be angry or guilty without letting these feelings ruin your life. You may think that your life is ruined anyhow and who cares, but anger and guilt turned inward can destroy your self-worth faster than anything. Take time to sort through these feelings and acknowledge them, then let them go.

Know that when anyone says, "It'll take time," we can nod and try to accept this as part of our getting through these days, months and years.

But don't forget that someday you will take the time to help someone else and that time will be the most satisfying time of all.

Therese

LYNN BENNETT BLACKBURN, PH.D., AUTHOR OF TIMOTHY DUCK,
CLASS IN ROOM 44, AND I KNOW I MADE IT HAPPEN. SHE WORKS
IN MISSOURI WITH CHILDREN WHO HAVE NEUROLOGICAL DISORDERS.
HER SON, D. J., DIED AT AGE 6 OF CANCER.

Dear Parents,

When my son died, it felt like a hole had opened up in me. In the days immediately following his death, friends and relatives formed a retaining wall around the hole, keeping the emptiness from growing and spreading. Then it became time to get on with things; time to learn to live with the hole.

DEAR
PARENTS
~
A
Collection
of Letters
to
Bereaved
Parents
~
12

I returned to work and discovered three kinds of people there. Some couldn't see the hole. They expected me to work and relate just like before. Some seemed afraid of the hole, as if they got to close, the hole would consume them. Luckily, there also were people who knew the hole was there, could give me opportunities to talk about it.

In the first few months, trips to the cemetery were very important. When I sat at his grave, for a few moments the missing piece seemed there. The hole seemed filled. Gradually, visits to the cemetery gave way to moments of remembering. Memories of time were shared. What was in my heart and my mind became more important than what was left at the cemetery.

The hole is much smaller now. It will never totally go away. The fact that he is gone can never be balanced by the memories that remain.

My son knew other children with cancer who died. He often asked as their death approached if their family would be OK. I always told him they would. My daughter asked many questions about how you survive the death of someone close. I wrote a story, **Timothy Duck**, to help them understand. Its message is that you take time to grieve, but life goes on. Listening to that story read at his funeral, I knew we all faced the challenge of making life go on.

We have all changed. Life has gone on. The good times and good feelings are still there. Sometimes the hole grows large for a few hours or days. The loss of a friend to suicide and the death of another friend's son on the same day made my sense of loss grow. My daughter understood. She called for Timothy Duck, then was Timothy with a waddle and a quack and a reminder about life going on. This keeps the hole in perspective.

Life goes on supported by the people who can see the hole, support you in moments when the loss overwhelms, yet help you reach beyond to what has not been lost. Life goes on and it can be good.

Lynn

JUDY OSGOOD IS THE AUTHOR/EDITOR OF A MEDITATION SERIES FOR BEREAVED PARENTS, THE WIDOWED AND THE DIVORCED. HER SON, ERIC, 16, DIED FROM A TOXIC REACTION TO CHEMOTHERAPY DRUGS.

Dear Parents,

Looking back to the days surrounding my son's death, two things stand out in my memory as being enormously helpful. Both were comments to my husband and I, in letters from friends.

The first one was from a woman who lost an infant daughter twenty years prior to the time she wrote to us.

In her letter she said that if our son's short life was to have special meaning, it was up to us to add it for him. She didn't tell us how; she challenged us to find a way to do it.

Instinctively we knew she was right, that he could live on through us, and that she had given us a key for healing. Our job was to create our own formula for rebuilding our lives and extending his impact on the world. And so we began the life-long process of 'doing this one for Eric.'

Sometimes that has taken the form of fulfilling his dreams. Eric loved to climb mountains, so each time we scale a new one we make a note in the summit registry that 'this climb is for our son, Eric, who has climbed the highest summit and waits for us in Heaven.'

But more often, adding meaning to his life takes the form of doing something for others, or something creative in his name. Whatever the form the result is the same, something positive is brought out of the most terrible negative in our lives.

The other letter was from a priest who shared the following quotation:

Be patient toward all that is unsolved in
your heart and try to love the questions themselves. (Rilke)

When it arrived we were reeling under the impact of the why questions that continually whirled through our heads. How? I asked myself, could I possibly love those horrible questions? But even as I did so, I realized that a how had replaced a why and another step toward healing had been taken.

How can you add meaning to your child's life? How can you love the questions without answers? How can you bring something positive out of the most terrible negative in your life?

The answer, and the healing, is in the searching and the doing.

Judy

Dear Parents,

We share an agony of life--a child's death. My daughter, Linda, age 3, died over 40 years ago, and in my memory-feelings it was only yesterday.

DEAR
PARENTS
~
A
Collection
of Letters
to
Bereaved
Parents
~
14

I have always wanted to be a wisdom person, learning the lessons that come through life's encounters with the passages of time. You have heard, "Time will heal your grief." Neat sayings like that really got under my skin 40 years ago. There were others: "It was God's will." "At least she didn't have to suffer long." "I admire how strong you are." Oh, how I hated being strong, crying within, holding my screams, taking care of everyone else! I thought this was my task. I would grow to resent the questions, "How is your wife?" No one asked, "How are YOU?!!?" Now, years later, I know that awkward questions and neat sayings are a product of awkward times for relatives and friends. Such good intentions do not penetrate the barriers we build to protect ourselves from ruin during our pain. I hope you receive support that opens the gate of healing rather than well-intentioned babble that misses your heart.

When Linda died I did what a man did then. I was strong, took care of my family, went back to work. My granite was polished, smooth and strong. For a man it was three days off, then back to work. I have met other fathers who suffered their grief in a dark secret place, appearing as if nothing had happened. Fifteen years later I opened the valve that kept my 'Linda grief' so tightly shut within me. I discovered it was not the lack of words or understanding from other people that inhibited my grieving, it was my unwillingness to risk expressing my own feelings. I discovered it is not TIME that heals; the healing was within me, waiting for release, to talk and share my feelings, risk opening myself to another person, to face the truth and that would let me be free to grieve. This was not a good experience nor a bad experience; for me it became a rich experience which enabled me to face life with the confidence that living is rich and meaningful.

My wish for you is that you will find your own time, your own courage to face your grief. When you hear someone say, "Give yourself time," remember time is there for you to grasp--or it will pass you by. When you hear, "Get over your grief," or "Work it through," remember the death of your child is not something to get over or work through. Linda will always be a very special part of me, in my memory and feelings. She remains my three-year-old. She touched my life for three beautiful years and I cherish her and am delighted for the time we shared. My life has been richer because I had the privilege of being her father. My wish for you, dear parent, is that you will take your grief for your own, knowing you will always cherish your child--in your memory and your heart.

Marv

Sudden Death

Looking back, I can see that the momentary pause in living

was the only way I could have survived my child's death.

My husband said that if it weren't for the blessedness of shock,

there would be no bereaved parents.

Our hearts, unprotected, could never stand such mortal wounds.

MARTHA CLARK

Dear Parents,

Sharing life with Jeffrey has been the greatest joy and the greatest sorrow for me. When he died, I had moments of incredible peace remembering the night he was born, slipping into this world so easily. . . likewise slipping out of it so easily.

I believe Jeffrey was a gift to teach me and others about loving and living. He had taken care of me, understood me, and walked with me through all kinds of experiences. He was mellow and taught ways of peace. He often seemed so near and yet so distant at other times, almost as if he had one part of himself here, another in a far off place. Jeffrey will always be cherished and honored for who he was here, and for who he has become to me since.

The transition of giving up the physical person, Jeffrey, as we had known him, was a long and heartbreaking experience. Not being able to ever again feel the warmth of his body was devastating to me, and for weeks I would feel actual pain in my body as I ached for him.

As time went on, I started to experience Jeffrey in different ways. A spiritual presence became more and more apparent, which gave me a secret joy and comfort. I realized that no one could take that away from me! Now I can be in touch with his presence at will. I consider that, as well as going on with life in a positive way, my own personal healing.

I have twin daughters who also miss their brother and try to understand why and how Jeffrey left us. They, too, experience Jeffrey's presence in many ways, and he remains a strong part of their lives.

At this point, I have developed a quiet, honest, and strong sense of appreciation about the here and now, and I strive to connect each day with love and reflection. That is really all we have, and there are no guarantees about anyone or anything around us. But for me, what is understood is that I need to continue to keep trusting life, myself and what I know now.

I would wish that no parent ever had to experience the death of their child. But I also know that there are always treasures to keep, and lessons to learn from loss. At the same time, I will continue to weep and feel real pain for any parent whose child dies. That is my truth and experience as Jeffrey Stead's mother.

Kathie

DEAR
PARENTS
~
A
Collection
of Letters
to
Bereaved
Parents
~
16

CANDY LIGHTNER IS THE FOUNDER OF **MADD**, MOTHERS AGAINST DRUNK DRIVING.
HER TEENAGE DAUGHTER, CARI, WAS KILLED BY A DRUNK DRIVER.

Dear Parents,

You have just experienced the worst loss anyone can possibly imagine. Right now
you may doubt the existence of God or at least a just and fair God. You have a right
to those feelings. Your child is dead and you feel helpless. It's silly for me to tell
you that "time heals all wounds"--because right now there is no sense of time. You
feel like someone just dropped 5,000 pounds on your chest and there are days when
you cannot function. You'll question your own mentality and wonder if you are
going senile. I can only tell you that this is grief--the mourning process--an evil
necessity if we are going to heal.

Ignore the insensitive remarks from family and friends for they simply cannot understand your pain. Grieving is unique. We each mourn in our own way. Cry when
you need to and don't worry what others think. Don't apologize for feeling miserable, angry or despondent. Share your feelings whenever there is that need. Talk
about your child if it makes you feel better. If friends try and change the subject
explain how they can help you through this difficult and tragic time.

Try not to feel guilty. So many of us experience the 'if only' syndrome--if only I had
picked him up after school--if only I hadn't yelled at her--you are not responsible for
their death. Chances are you did everything you could at the time to love and nur-
ture. WE can't live our lives with our children as if their death is imminent.

Set aside time to grieve. I didn't. I wish I had. To quote Samuel Johnson, "While
grief is fresh, every attempt to divert only irritates," I grieved 5 and 1/2 years after
Cari was killed by a drunk driver. The pain was just as intense as if she had died
the day before.

The important thing to remember is that you are not alone. Others have gone before
you: unfortunately, more will follow. Take care of yourself. You are very important.
Do not add any stress to your life if you can avoid it. Surround yourselves with
loved ones.

All the letters you will read are from those who have suffered your pain and survived. It was not easy. I still miss Cari, and sometimes I think she is the lucky one.

Candy

ANDREA GAMBILL IS THE EDITOR AND CREATOR OF **BEREAVEMENT MAGAZINE, A MAGAZINE OF HOPE AND HEALING.** HER DAUGHTER DIED IN AN AUTOMOBILE ACCIDENT.

Dear Parents,

Ask any bereaved parent, and they will fairly shriek the answer: "The death of a child is the worst loss!" That may not be entirely fair to some other bereaved folks, but it reveals the depth of the pain when parents must say one final goodbye to a beloved child.

DEAR
PARENTS
~
A
Collection
of Letters
to
Bereaved
Parents
~
18

The relationship between parents and child is unique. It may be the closest thing we will ever know of the love of God for His children. Other kinds of love relationships are often more complex and negotiable: "If you love me, I will love you back." "If you meet my needs, I will love you." "I will love you until you disappoint me" – but parental love is unconditional, unwavering and fierce.

That unique quality of love is undoubtedly why grief is so severe when a child dies. Grief is the price we pay for loving, and the intensity of grieving is directly related to the intensity of bonding. We declare that we are not supposed to outlive our children, but we always knew that some children do die–we just never thought any of them would be ours!

This is a difficult wound to heal. It takes time – a lot of time – and even then we never "get over it." With a lot of nurturing, love, compassion, support, patience and understanding, we eventually get through it. Gradually, we begin to discover new ways to define our lives and new goals and missions to bring another kind of meaning to our existence. While the pain does not remain at the same intensity forever, it will always lurk in the background, and many simple "triggers" can set off a new episode of grief's expression. Each time there is a major change in our life experiences, we again become vulnerable to upsurges of grief.

While we never forget, and we never stop loving and missing, life can become meaningful again. Eventually, most of us come to the place where what we want most is to become living memorials – keeping alive the memory of the child who died and becoming a credit to that memory. Before my daughter died in 1976, I was a smug, born-again, fundamentalist Christian Bible teacher who knew all the answers. Now, I am just a bereaved mother who knows all the questions. I've improved a lot over the years, and I like me better now! God likes me better, too. I'm a lot wiser, gentler and more understanding and compassionate than I was in my old life. I'd give anything if Judy hadn't died to teach me that, but since I didn't have a vote in the matter, I'm grateful for the improvement and the education.

For me, it was a terrible tragedy that such a promising young life could be cut short at seventeen years, but the greater tragedy would have been if that suffering had been tossed away on the trash heap of despair. I needed to know that something good and profoundly positive could come from such a terrible loss. It's been a long, slow process and I've had to learn to forgive myself for a lot of things, but the grief journey has produced a better me.

My belief system assures me that one day Judy and I will be reunited in a new kind of loving relationship in a different time dimensions, but just in case they can see from where they are, I want her to be able to nudge the kid next to her and point at me proudly saying, "That's my mom!"

Andrea

SAUNI WOOD IS THE AUTHOR OF **MOMMA MOCKINGBIRD.**
MAMMA MOCKINGBIRD SHOWS US HOW TO FIND YOUR SONG WHEN ONE OF YOUR CHILDREN DIES.

Dear Parents,

Though I don't know you, I ache for you. I cry with you in your loss. You might wonder why? In some mysterious way, since my son died, I feel connected to any parent who has suffered the loss of a child. Perhaps it is because the pain of loss remains deep in the marrow of my bones so I need to reach out to another in understanding and in support. You know of my pain. I know of yours. I ache for you and I cry with you.

DEAR
PARENTS
~
*A
Collection
of Letters
to
Bereaved
Parents*
~
20

Each of us is so unique that the way we process our grief may be different from one another. When I first heard the terrible news, I felt as if a sharp knife had pierced through my body, stoped me in my tracks, pushed me to my knees and left me with just enough breath to wail. And wail, I did! My husband, the father of our son wept, but mostly in the dark of night. Our son's sister and brothers did what they needed to do. Tears and more tears were allowed to flow openly. Anger, resentment, guilt, helplessness, fatigue, remorse were in our own way, in our own time. The sharing helped enormously, yet we knew that the mountain of grief had to be climbed by each of us, one step at a time, one day at a time, one week at a time, one month at a time, one year at a time.

The journey of healing goes on for me. It will always go on. How could in not? To lose a child is a terrible thing. . . a child so special, so wonderful, so loved. . .no longer among us to touch, to hug, to hear from, to share with. . .and yet he will always be with us forever and ever. Miracles occur in spite of it all, inexplicable miracles. . . a story that comes "through the wind" as I walked through the mountains grieving for my son. . .a story that had the healing powers for me. In the story, Mama Mockingbird lost her song after she lost her son. On a journey to find her song again, she discovers the secret to find it. A miracle! Wonders of wonder!

I'd like to sit longer with you, "be" with you. I'd listen if that would be helpful. I'm comfortable with silence, as well. And should you want to be alone. . .I'll honor that. When you are alone, maybe my story will help. . .and maybe you will be blessed with a story of your own. One assurance I have for you from my own personal experience is that in time it will be easier. Of course, you'll never get over it. Nor should you! But you will learn to live with the loss. . .and that's a miracle in itself. Give yourself time, precious time.

Sincerely yours,

Sauni Wood

SUSAN EVANS IS THE AUTHOR OF, LATER COURTNEY, A MOTHER SAYS GOODBYE,
A JOURNAL THROUGH SUSAN'S GRIEF AFTER THE DEATH OF HER DAUGHTER,
COURTNEY, AGE 22, IN AN AUTOMOBILE ACCIDENT.

Dear Parents,

I wish I could send you some hope. When my first child was born, I needed other mothers to show me what to do. When that same child died, I then needed bereaved mothers.

Grief is a lonely place. In spite of what some books would lead you to believe no two people have quite the same experience there. I can tell you that I exercise every day to stay balanced and keep a journal where I can ask the "why" questions that have no answers. That might not be your style. Or I can tell you that I've cut back on the projects I pursue to conserve energy and spend more time alone. But I know other parents who do the opposite. There is no formula.

When Courtney died, I was sure I would as well. The loss seemed too great to bear. I think every parent feels that way, yet remarkably most of us survive. I've gotten through some very dark days just knowing that Vicki who lost her son Neil is going to law school and that Karen went on to have a third child after losing her daughter. I figure if they can go on living so can I.

It's been five years since I lost my child. I no longer cry every day, but the sadness is always with me. how could it not be? She was a part of me in life. She continues to be a part of me in death. That's my new reality. I'm learning to live with it. I pray you can find hope in that. I do.

With Love,
Susan

Dear Parents,

There is no more difficult time than the one you are experiencing, for the loss of a child is the unthinkable becoming a reality. I don't think it matters whether that child was an infant, a teen-ager, or an adult; the grief is just as wrenching, the loss is as painful and the sense of disbelief as overwhelming. As parents, we see our children as both present and future beings. When that future is lost, the pain is incredible.

I know that in my own case, the pain drove me inward, to a place I'd never been within myself. As difficult as that journey was, I returned from it with a knowledge that I had not previously had. That knowledge was an awareness of the strength, previously unrecognized, within us. It may come to you in the form of spiritual beliefs or in the support of friends and family. It may be a need to make a contribution to others who are suffering a similar loss. You may find that there are times when you must be strong enough to let others take care of you. No matter what form your strength takes, have faith that you do have it.

I used to become frustrated, waiting for the hurt to go away. It was months before I realized that I was waiting for the wrong thing. People would say, "Time heals" and I would wait for the healing to occur. I realized eventually that it was not time that would heal, for healing is not a passive event. It was my own strength that would have to propel me through the difficult times and take me to a place that was, once again, livable. It was extremely hard work.

I will will never forget the incredible generosity of those who helped me. I will never forget the incredible pain of losing the son that I loved. I will never forget the young man he was and could have been. But, life is not what could have been, life is what is. Losses of the magnitude of the death of your child give you a choice. You can choose to make the death your life or you can choose to make your life meaningful in spite of the death. You can use the strength you find inside you to do thing you never thought possible. You can honor the memory of your loved one by being someone they could have been proud of. . . no matter what. You are stronger than you think. Trust yourself enough to cry when you need to, remember when you want to, and live again. You really can.

Linda

DEAR
PARENTS
~
A
Collection
of Letters
to
Bereaved
Parents
~
22

KELLY OSMONT WROTE MORE THAN SURVIVING, TAKING CARE OF YOURSELF WHILE YOU GRIEVE. KELLY'S SON AND ONLY CHILD, AARON, 19, DIED DURING HIS 5TH SURGERY AFTER A HORSE KICKED HIM IN HIS STOMACH.

Hi,

If I had my way, the first thing I would do, instead of sending you a letter, is call you and ask when we could visit in your place. Going out is so hard at the beginning. When you answered the door, the next thing I would do is wrap my arms around you and give you a big, long hug. Then we'd sit down. Instead of coffee, I would suggest we drink hot water with a squirt of lemon juice. Early grief brings such anxieties and coffee becomes a negative stimulant. During this difficult time, I want you to stay healthy.

Then I would ask, "How was your day yesterday?" . . . then, we would sit while you talked. When you cried, I would wait until you had finished. Oh, how frustrated I used to get when people would push tissue boxes toward me, or pat my hand and make some trite remark like, "There must have been a reason." Crying is so good for one's soul and health. I did not get sick once during my first two years of mourning. I think because I cried a lot, exercised and slept when I needed to . . . including naps on a couch at the office.

Later, I would suggest we take a walk. I want you to get some exercise, for again, you are ripe for colds, flues and depressions. Exercise is great for depressions!

I would ask you to tell me things about your child who died. What he liked doing, her special qualities and things that used to bug you. I would ask you to show me pictures of your child and tell me about where they were taken and all the stories behind them.

All this time I know my heart would ache for you. I would continue to reach out to you physically, for I want you to know I am here for you and you are loved. And that's all I can do for you . . . listen to your heartache, hold you when you're feeling vulnerable, and assure you that you will feel better, very slowly . . . someday in the far future. But you needn't rush it. Take your time. I am not afraid of your pain and your tears. Late that afternoon, as we hugged before I left, I hope another gift to you would be the knowledge that I and others have survived, and so can you.

But since we can only communicate in his written form, show THIS letter to your friends, so they can do for you what by distance, I am unable to do.

My heart goes out to you.

Kelly

PAULA CARLSON IS A MOTHER IN PORT COQUITLAM, BRITISH COLUMBIA.
HER OLDEST DAUGHTER, DEANNE, DIED ON MOTHER'S DAY, 1986.

Dear Parents,

Deanne was 16 years old when she was in a tragic car accident. After being in a coma for one week, she died a brain death. It was Mother's Day.

In the first moment of truth, when you are told your child is dead, there's a feeling of disbelief! Shock sets in very quickly! You become a zombie, numb to everyone around you. You live in a cocoon-like state for months. This cocoon protects you from the knife in the heart, the reality of it all.

DEAR
PARENTS
~
A
Collection
of Letters
to
Bereaved
Parents
~
24

It seems like forever that you're in the dazed, numb, unreal world. Then the layers finally start unwrapping, and fearfully you let them. The pain of reality sets in. The unbelievable has happened. My child has died! My heart is torn to shreds. My body is screaming. My mind is crazed! My world has come to a sudden crashing stop.

The question is always present on my mind. Why?! How could this possibly have happened. The anger is ever so deep, so strong, so frightening. Will I ever let go of it?

Some of us let the feelings happen. We feel the pain as we try to trudge on, still dazed. As we pull ourselves out of the quicksand, it is still difficult to move and especially hard to concentrate. Memory keeps failing us. Others move right into another world, a world of make-believe. The pain is just too much to bear.

After awhile the shock wears off, like an ice cube melting. You're able to cry, and cry, and cry, and maybe even rant and rave. You do this for a long time, crying yourself a river, wondering if it can or will ever stop.

Somehow, one day you get through the day, or maybe only half of it, without crying. Slowly, those days turn into weeks. For me, it has been over a year since my daughter died, but my tears have not been absent for a whole month yet.

Life may never be normal again, but there are ways of coping. They come so slowly. It's like learning to walk all over again, only this time in a different direction.

Expectations of others become hard to bear. Family, friends and people around you think that after a certain amount of time you should be back to your old self again. Not so! For me, my old self died with my child. My new self is a whole new personality. Others cannot comprehend this. We learn to stand alone; so very much alone. We are different people. Sometimes we can't even understand ourselves. Others may not accept this, and we go our own way, clinging to those who do understand.

One's health may be on the line. Doctors report that the immune system suffers drastically during mourning. With me, it seemed like my mind was in so much pain, it could take no more, so cast it into my body. A lot of unbelievable, mind-boggling physical things can happen. I knew it was important to eat properly and get lots of rest. I found that difficult to do as I wasn't hungry and I sure couldn't sleep.

Most important is finding a way to work through your grief. It may be talking a lot about your child, writing down feelings, talking to a grief counselor. When an over-whelming sense of loneliness, sadness or helplessness strikes me, I write. I can express more feelings on paper than I can with words. Whatever it may be, some form of therapy is truly needed.

The feelings that go along with the loss of a child are enough to destroy one's inner soul, if not dealt with in some healthy way. If ever there's a time to let someone support you, this is the time.

We can't hide from the pain and reality forever. To face it and feel it are the only ways of helping yourself through it. There is no easier, softer way. It is like a never-ending roller coaster ride . . . a living nightmare.

I often hear Deanne's voice or picture her standing in a doorway. Even hallucina-tions are not out of the ordinary when you are grieving. At one time I had a vision of my daughter in a lovely white gown being lifted gently towards heaven. A very peaceful look was on her face. We learn to be respectful of life's innermost teach-ings. We have been given a choice, to learn and grow from a painful experience. A whole new path awaits us.

There will always be a special place in my heart for Deanne. I will always search for her lovely face in a crowd. She was a beautiful, happy, loving, giving child whom I will love and miss forever. Although life is painful, I will live it. I have another beautiful, loving daughter, Denise, who is a miracle. She lives on the 'hopes and dreams of medical science.' If she can tolerate life's irony and still smile, then why can't I? The passing of time has become a new friend. Now, after 17 months, I can say yes, time does help. There is a light at the end of my tunnel.

Paula

ADINA WROBLESKI WAS A PROFESSIONAL SPEAKER AND WRITER SPECIALIZING IN PUBLIC EDUCATION ABOUT SUICIDE AND SUICIDE GRIEF. HER DAUGHTER, LYNN, KILLED HERSELF.

Dear Parents,

My daughter, Lynn, killed herself. I have been where you are now. I know how badly it hurts. I know that you feel the most terrible aloneness of your life. It is normal for you to feel desperately unhappy, angry, guilty, frightened and out of control. You wouldn't feel terrible if you hadn't loved your child so much.

DEAR
PARENTS
~
*A
Collection
of Letters
to
Bereaved
Parents*
~
26

Most people who kill themselves had depression--usually unrecognized and undiagnosed. People who have depression have an illness. Chemicals get out of balance in their brains, which regulate how they think, feel and behave. No amount of love and caring, or trying to build up their self-esteem could have altered their misconception that their situation was hopeless.

Please don't let anyone tell you how you should feel. People will say that the death of a child by suicide is the 'worst' thing that can happen, that you will 'never' get over it. Don't believe them; these are the voices of the taboo and stigma on suicide. This is part of the extra burden you will have as a suicide survivor. Others don't hear gasps of shock as we do when we tell how our child died. Others don't hear gross jokes and ridicule about the manner of their child's death. That's extra for us.

You may feel bewildered and stunned; go over and over the events leading up to the death; feeling that somehow--if you had done one last thing--you might have saved your child; you may be fearful and anxious about yourself and the rest of your family. These things, and more, are normal reactions after a suicide death.

You will survive the suicide death of your child because you have to, but you have the choice about how you will survive. You have gotten through the days since your child died--the worst that can happen already has happened. It cannot get worse. You have been through the worst, and you have survived.

The next several months will gradually get easier, but it probably won't feel that way day by day. It will be up and down. It helps to look back over a week or a month and compare. Recognize your small victories. Death leaves a scar that we always have, and we will feel pain from it through our lives, but the intense pain you feel now will gradually get better; the pain won't be there forever. Ultimately for suicide survivors, it is not so much how our children died, as that they died.

Keep in mind that you are a good person, and you deserve to be happy again. You are going to be alright, but it will not be easy, especially at first. I still miss Lynn, but I know she went as far as she could, and that she would have stayed with us if she could. Some people, like your child and my Lynn, have to leave before the play is over. Be good to yourself.

Adina

LINDSAY HARMER IS CO-FOUNDER OF THE COMPASSIONATE FRIENDS OF AUSTRALIA. HIS SON, RHYS, DIED EN ROUTE TO THE HOSPITAL FOLLOWING AN AUTOMOBILE ACCIDENT.

Dear Parents,

I know the extreme pain you are feeling. I once stood by the hospital bed of my wife, Margaret, waiting for her to regain consciousness and to tell her that our loved and only son of 11, Rhys, had died in the same ambulance as his unconscious mother . . . neither knowing that the other was there. One moment Margaret was a mother, loving life and with her family intact; the next moment, a car crash . . . a death . . . and no place nor time to say those vital goodbyes.

I, father and husband, had been completely ignored. I was left at the roadside following the accident to get back to the hospital as best I could; not in the ambulance with my loved ones but in a police van.

There was so much unfinished business, to run from or to work through. There was so much grief and trauma. Ever so slowly we shared with one another, painfully, gently, to become new persons. . . living and yet searching for our new land of love and acceptance. And I know the huge effort of becoming a new person has already begun for you. I also know, from my own slow journey of 15 years since Rhys' death, it will be possible from the fires of suffering to forge a new life and a new world . . . but ever so slowly.

I know that with courage and determination you will make it through. You will survive this torture and become more positive and compassionate, more caring and loveable, more aware and more grateful to your own family and friends. There IS the hope of a new day in the future without this horrible, overwhelming and disorienting pain . . . but the pain is natural and normal for how you feel now.

The feelings, the deep, intense feelings are normal and OK. You need to become familiar with them all. They are really your friends and need to be understood, identified and treasured as the expression of love and the pain of loving and losing. They are the deepest feelings possible in a human being, and they can come and go with amazing frequency.

Be easy on yourself. Don't try to be a perfect griever, always showing your faith and wearing a mask. Don't spend precious energy on 'show.' Remember that time is a friend also. It gives us space to do the hard work of understanding the reality of our loss, enables us to cope, face it and choose how we want to work with it in order to live once more. No matter what pain you are experiencing, take it one day at a time. If at all possible, attend a support group. The Compassionate Friends are everywhere and willing to walk you through your pain.

Above all, I wish you well.

Lindsey

Elaine Stillwell is the author of Sweet Memories, a hands-on crafts book for grieving children. Her two oldest children, 21 year old Denis and 19 year old Peggy, died in a car accident. She is founder of the Rockville Centre, NY Chapter of The Compassionate Friends and former TCF NYS Regional Coordinator.

Dear Parents,

When the excruciating pain goes down to your toes and your heart feels like it is in a vice, what do you do? How do you get up in the mourning? My heart broke when my beautiful 19 year old daughter, Peggy, was killed instantly in a freak car accident. Four days later, the day after we buried her, her brother Denis, my first-born, died from the same accident and we had two funerals in one week.

When the last care-giver left our home the evening of Denis' funeral, my husband and I looked at each other and wondered how we, and our remaining child, would survive. We didn't have a clue and had no idea of the long road ahead of us as we attempted to reweave our family tapestry.

As I faced the heartbreaking chore of sorting out my children's possessions while shedding many tears, it upset me to toss out their college I.D. cards, social security cards, library and credit cards, and drivers license. It dawned on me how easily they might become erased from the memories of friends and loved ones. I didn't want them erased! I vowed that would never happen. I guess you could say I started a crusade. That became a primary motivating factor for me. That idea got me out of bed in the morning/ mourning. I was on fire to tell the world about my children, even though I had limited energy and no definite plan how to do it. I talked about them to everybody, whether I was on the grocery line, bank queue, airplane, or sitting in a doctor's office. Now, people who never met Peggy and Denis tell me that they feel they know them. Do you know what that does for my heart?

On days when I was tempted to stay in bed and pull the covers over my head, trying to run away from my pain, I wondered what my children would think of that. Not much, I figured. How I wanted them to continue to be proud of me, rather than embarrassed, every time they looked down on me from above! I wanted them to smile big grins, pop their buttons, and exclaim, "That's my mom!" That vision fueled me to keep going. I kept praying to Peggy and Denis to give me strength on my journey and they never let me down. We were a team for survival!

Then, I realized that I did not want to waste this wonderful love I have for my Peggy and Denis. By sharing this special love with others, by reinvesting it, I could keep Peggy's and Denis' memories alive while helping others. In that expression of love, I was really blossoming, too, for I found helping is healing.

I think my crusade has been successful! My children are dearly remembered and I enjoy the bonus of a meaningful life. Look into your hearts, dear parents, and find your motivating factors.

Elaine

KAREN FULCHER LIVES IN NORTH EASTON, MASSACHUSETTS.
HER DAUGHTER, KARENSUE, WAS KILLED IN AN AUTOMOBILE ACCIDENT.

Dear Parents,

My Karensue survived in a coma 34 days before she died . . . the longest days of my life . . . I say survived. Her life and mine stopped with the phone call every parent dreads. "Your daughter . . . an accident . . . in critical condition . . . in intensive care."

My first reaction was hysteria--unusual for me. I handle crises with strength, courage and positive thinking. Why did I lose control? Why could I not think clearly? I remember through those days I needed everyone who cared for her to know how special she was . . . that she was loved more than life. . . that they had to save her. Days went by and I knew from their faces that we were losing the battle.

When she died I stayed in control, went through the paces, did what was expected. I was in shock. The shock began the day of the phone call and it was months before I realized this was happening. It was not a dream. She is dead. How I hate that word!

I went to a bereaved parents groups and realized I didn't want to see parents who were surviving--who were handling their loss. I rationalized they couldn't have loved their child as much as I did or they would be dead themselves. I knew I couldn't live long with this pain; how could they?

What I have learned is, don't be afraid . . . of losing your mind, of contemplating suicide, of knowing your friends will get tired of hearing you talk about it, or see you crying or all the other feelings you will have these next months and years.

I have also reached the following conclusions--there is no recipe for grief, no timetable, no cure. You can cry for days, weeks, months and when you think you are OK you have a 'sneak attack.' I know I had a memory before Karensue died. Now I try to remember a conversation 5 minutes old. Talk about your child. I talked about her when she was alive, why not now? If it makes people uncomfortable, that's their problem. Talk, cry, yell.

Find a group if possible, and find strength there. I went back to my group and became one of those parents who were coping, handling, going on.

All of her life, whenever she had a problem or a mountain to climb, I always told Karensue, "Go ahead, Hon. You can do it. Just dig in and try." If I can't make it through this, then all that good advice would have been a lie, and her life was not a lie. Know my prayers are with you, too, to make it through. And don't question. There are no answers in this life. But, oh, when I get to heaven--the answers He must give to me for all of this!

Karen

BETHANY HOMEYER'S SON, MICHAEL, DIED AT AGE 18 AFTER CLIMBING OUT OF AN AUTOMOBILE WIN
WHILE THE CAR WAS GOING 65 MILES AN HOUR. BOTH MICHAEL AND THE DRIVER HAD BEEN DRINF
MICHAEL WAS WIND-SURFING ON THE HOOD OF THE CAR WHEN HE FELL AND LATER DIED.

Dear Parents,

There's nothing you can do. What I have found is it's going to take a long time before
even think you're thinking normally. You may not think you're in shock but you are. A
know only too well, the hardest time is after the funeral when the reality begins to set in
you're trying to figure out whether or not this is real. For a long time you just won't be
it's happened.

DEAR
PARENTS
~
*A
Collection
of Letters
to
Bereaved
Parents*
~
30

It was important to me that my child be remembered. People went on with their daily lif
my son was gone. How could they go on living when my world was shattered?

Words won't help. There are no words. Hugs help. Time helps. It does ease the pair
literally tears at your heart. Know that will ease a little. Know also that the healing go
forever. Life as you knew it will never be the same, so you find a new life. Believe tha
will.

Michael was our last one at home. My empty nest came much sooner than expected. W
Michael's room as it had been and when the kids came home they would sleep there.
protective of Michael's things. I wanted so much to touch him, to hold him but I couldi
I would touch and hold this things.

My healing began the day I thought I was losing my sanity. I just told God, *God, you hc
take this I can't handle it any more. Take it back.* I was in real pain and I didn't want
here. I felt guilty. I wondered where I had failed. Could I have chained him to his bec
not let him go anywhere? No. He was 18 and he made his choice that night and paid
with his life. I had hit bottom. After I gave it back to God, I felt my first moment of pea
knew Michael was all right. Your child is all right, too.

I felt there was some kind of plan for me. As long as I was talking too much to God, I asked that I be made a tool and used. Michael was my nature child and I went outside into my garden and started gardening again. Digging in the dirt, I remembered reading about a man who was raising butterflies and releasing them. I started researching the butterfly and the reality of the symbol of life after death really touched me. The butterfly was emerging on the other side as a whole new being. Michael was emerging on the other side, too.

I can't get closer to God than when I'm playing in the dirt. I started raising the plants needed to feed the butterflies and gradually I moved into raising the butterflies. The lives the butterflies have touched have meant so much to me. While many go to brides, they also go to funerals and memorials and Centering's camp for grieving children.

Next time you see a butterfly, know that your child is still there, just in a different form and beautiful and given a choice, they don't want to come back. Your child is beautiful and safe, Dear Parents, just as mine is.

Bethany

MARTHA CLARK'S DAUGHTER, SHERRY, WAS KILLED IN AN ACCIDENT NEAR HER COLLEGE. "THERE WAS NOTHING IN MY LIFE THAT PREPARED ME FOR THE HORROR OF MY CHILD'S DEATH."

Dear Parents,

I know how badly you must hurt. And there is nothing I can do to take away the pain. You have lost a child--a part of yourself--and the reality of that loss will be with you for as long as you live.

When I learned that my precious Sherry had been killed, I was so stunned--so shaken--that my 'living' just stopped! And I was confused to see others move on without me, doing the things we take for granted as being necessary to do. How can they cook, clean, mow lawns and send children off to school when Sherry has been killed, I wondered. I was sure those normal-like days were lost to me forever. And for a very long time, they were.

DEAR
PARENTS
~
A
Collection
of Letters
to
Bereaved
Parents
~
32

Looking back from a 6-year perspective, I can see that the momentary pause in living was the only way I could have survived my child's death. My husband, Cecil, said that if it weren't for the blessedness of shock, there would be no bereaved parents! Our hearts, unprotected, could never ever stand such mortal wounds.

You must be feeling the pain of those wounds now. How I wish you were really here and could share with me about your child. I ache to know the seemingly unimportant details that only another grieving mother would want to know. Did he smile when you come into his room each morning? Did she enjoy being cuddled in your arms? What was his favorite thing to do? Who was her best friend? Nothing helps grieving parents more than to talk about their children. We learn very quickly to cherish the memories we have, for we can no longer add to those memories.

Of all the things I could say to you, that is what I would stress the most. Talk about your child every day. Set aside a remembering time when you search your heart and bring every memory out into the open. Laugh if you need to, cry if you must, don't be afraid to get angry even if that anger is toward your child, sigh over hopes and grieve over dreams that will never be fulfilled. Don't be afraid to live your grief! After several months, you may discover that the remembering times don't need to last so long, or even occur every day, for you to be able to pick up some of your old activities and, at least, become a part-time participant in life.

Someday, dear friend, your memories will help make you whole again, but be patient with yourself. There is no timetable for grieving. It takes a long time to discover that the love we shared with our children can never die. It takes even longer to realize that there are ways to grow through sorrow. Just know that my love and support will be with you as you begin your walk through grief.

In love and compassion,

Martha

Infant death

She would be ten now--

Perhaps too old for laps but not too old to be tucked in at night

and kissed and told not to let the bedbugs bite.

TERRY MORGAN

Dear Parents,

First off, I want to say I'm sorry. Your baby has died, and I feel helpless, knowing I can't take away your pain with those few words. Yet I need to say them . . . and you, most likely, need to hear them said. Often.

DEAR
PARENTS

~

*A
Collection
of Letters
to
Bereaved
Parents*

~

34

I'm writing as a parent who has experienced a stillbirth. In 1981, I delivered my fourth child, a son we named Jesse, at 22 weeks gestation. He was born dead, never to be seen or held by either parent. The hospital staff wanted to 'spare us' the unpleasantness of this tiny death, but unintentionally, left us without memories of our son. Without memories of Jesse, recovering has been lengthy and haunting. We struggled for years, coming to terms with the stark reality that we did nothing in the way of a memorial service, nothing to tell our loved ones how important he was.

I had a fantasy for months after the birth that people would acknowledge Jesse's existence and say, "I am sorry this has happened. It's terrible." But few ever did. Moreover, I needed to be reassured during the grief process that I was normal, not completely off the wall as I had believed for too many months. I needed validation, compassion, resources, comfort. I was so needy it overwhelmed me.

In addition to these personal needs, I had a greater need to change the system that discouraged us from seeing, holding or memorializing our son. Eventually, I was able to help satisfy this need through working with others and creating the Pregnancy and Infant Loss Center. Today, PILC is a nationally-recognized organization, a pioneer in the field of perinatal bereavement, and an institution advocating for bereaved parents and educating our care providers. It's heartening to see our success and, in a way, I'm fulfilling my needs in a positive way.

Again, I'm sorry this has happened. It's terrible. It's unfair. Your life will never be the same without your baby, but hopefully, someday your pain will not quite so razor-sharp, and your memories will be more sweet than bitter.

Susan

MARTHA WEGNER-HAY IS THE AUTHOR OF **EMBRACING LAURA, THE GRIEF AND HEALING FOL-
LOWING THE DEATH OF AN INFANT TWIN.** HER TWIN DAUGHTER, LAURA, DIED BEFORE BIRTH.

Dear Parents,

Let me start by telling you how very sorry I am to hear of your child's death. If I
could be with you now, I would tell you that as often as you needed to hear it,
because I know you don't hear it enough. You see, the loss you and I experienced
was unique. No one, with the possible exception of medical staff and close friends
and family, got to see your baby. (Maybe you didn't get to see your baby either).
And because of that, (and maybe for lots of other reasons we don't know), many
people will find it hard to acknowledge your loss, much less grieve with you.

But you and I know differently. We know that even if there was no body, or the
baby's body was very sick or very tiny, this was a living being. It was a part of your
family. The minute you found out you were pregnant, you became this child's parents, caring for it, preparing for it, loving it. Just as you rejoiced in it's life, so you
grieve deeply in it's death. So of course you feel sad, or course it's hard to imagine
feeling "normal" again. You are not crazy, even though you might feel that way.
Even though the world around you proceeds as if nothing has happened, you know
that you have lost your baby. You have a right, indeed, a need to grieve this precious one. And, for what it's worth, I am grieving with you.

At the same time, you have a right to feel joy, and that feeling will assert itself more
as the days go on, although I know that is impossible to believe right now. After the
loss of my twin daughter, Laura, I had to give myself permission to feel joy with my
remaining children, Christine and David. It felt disloyal to Laura when I allowed
myself to feel any happiness with them. But I learned that Laura understood, she
knew I needed to be there for my other children, and any happiness I felt with them
did not lessen the love I felt for her.

Finally, I hope you feel some pride. I hope you are proud of yourself for taking good
care of your baby while he/she was alive. and I hope you take pride in how you
honor your baby after his/her death. You honor your child by talking about him or
her, by crying, by keeping his/her memory alive. You are this baby's parents, and
you are and were able to give this baby the care and love it needs.

I'll close by letting you know that you are not alone, even though I know you probably feel that way. Soon you'll find others who have experienced such a terrible loss.
Softly, gently, these people will come into your life. The ones who can put their
hand on your shoulder, give you a hug, and look you in the eye and say, "I understand. I'm so sorry." If I were with you now, I would say that to you. Instead I'll
write it, and you know that right now you are in my thoughts and prayers.

With Love,

Martha

MARIE TEAGUE IS THE FOUNDER OF THE SOUTHERN CALIFORNIA
PREGNANCY AND INFANT LOSS CENTER.
SHE HAS EXPERIENCED THE DEATH OF THREE EXPECTED CHILDREN.

Dear Parents,

I can't begin to tell you how sorry I am to hear about your loss.
There are no words to express the sadness in my heart.
It's not fair that your baby had to die, just as it wasn't fair that mine died.
If I could hold you in my arms, rock you, and soothe your anguish,
 I would . . .

DEAR
PARENTS
~
A
Collection
of Letters
to
Bereaved
Parents
~
36

The pain you're feeling right now is so intense you believe it will never end, and you assume you'll never laugh or love again.

The pain will soften with time, and with 'grief work.' I like to tell parents that at the beginning, grief is like a blazing fire, and over time it burns down to glowing embers, and finally smoldering coals, still hot enough to ignite, yet warm and comforting if we're careful to treat them with respect and consideration. The 'colors' of grief are then the range of the colors of fire. You are in the vibrant red and orange phase . . . while I am only a memory beyond that golden glow.

Give yourself time to heal . . . experience all the stages and phases of grieving.
You'll someday find comfort in your baby's name, and in the memory.

Be an active griever. Read all you can on loss and grief, attend support group meetings, and develop a healthy selfishness. You, after all, know what you need to feel better. Demand it of your family and friends. If you long to hear people mention your baby by name, ask that they do so. If comments such as "you're young. You'll have other babies," send you into orbit, tell those person's they're not being helpful. Let those around you know that the only healthy way to deal with a loss is to deal with it, not detour around the hurt and pain.

You'll make it !

I know you will, because I did. I felt lost, alone, miserable and even suicidal at times. But I made it. And I'm happy now. I can meet the future and whatever it holds for me with the assurance that I can do anything. After all, I've survived the death of three very much loved and wanted children. And with me always are the memories of those three little ones . . . my stillborn Brian and two miscarried wee ones. . . to comfort me, encourage me and make me the kind of mother I always wanted to be, appreciative and reverent of all the gifts of life and love.

I share those gifts with you. I love you.

Marie

DENISE GLEASON'S SON, DANIEL, BORN WITH A BIRTH DEFECT, LIVED ONLY 9 HOURS.

Dear Parents,

I can still remember the shock and pain of sitting there 8 months pregnant as our doctor told us the baby I carried would die shortly after birth. How could he be sure--it must be a mistake--I refused to give up hope. Six more weeks I waited, prayed and grieved. Then came my labor, his delivery, a child born dying. I felt so hollow, empty and cheated of a future.

The following weeks I felt aimless, unable to focus and scattered. At first it was hard to go out in public. I felt transparent . . . as though everyone could see through me to my broken heart. Surely my body gave me away, that flabby, 'just delivered.' figure with no baby to justify it. My full breasts were an aching reminder hour by hour. It was painful to see a baby or a pregnant woman. I felt I should warn them of what could happen. The urge to curl up and hide was almost overwhelming.

Our two daughters were such a help getting through those rough days. Their visions of 'Gramma rocking baby Daniel in Heaven' helped.

Somehow each day I felt stronger and soon I could think of Daniel for brief periods without crying. Later I could even smile as I remembered our short hours together. This time will come for you also, I'm sure of it.

Physical exercise helped me. I guess it gave me a sense of control in one part of my life. It was also a 'super' out for my anger. I found anniversary dates and the next Christmas very difficult. We baked Daniel a birthday cake at 1 year and sang Happy Birthday. This was right for us.

I'm a changed person now, and I feel OK about that. At first those changes scared me, I wanted my 'old self' back, the self that didn't know such pain. Gone now is the innocence of pregnancy filled with joy. In its place is reality, some babies don't make it. I have a new appreciation of life now.

At our memorial service when I tried to thank a supporting friend who had also lost a baby, she said, "Don't thank me. Just pass is on." I thought she was crazy, me the helper? No way! I hurt too much.

Now as I visit with other grieving parents, I realize the changed me CAN pass on the caring. I guess that's Daniel's gift to me, proof that he lives on!

Denise

Dear Parents,

Coming home from the hospital without your child is very difficult. The child of your hopes and dreams will never BE. Your baby will always be a part of your life, but somehow different than what you had planned. As you now meet with family and friends, some of the things they say may seem insensitive and even cruel. Things like . . . "You can have another baby--there must have been something wrong with the child--don't think about it." Try to be patient with them. They don't really understand your loss, and they really don't mean to offend you. Some people may even avoid you. Realize they really just don't know what to say to you.

DEAR
PARENTS
~
A
Collection
of Letters
to
Bereaved
Parents
~
38

You and your partner may grieve differently. Be good to your relationship, and even through it may seem that one of you hurts more sometimes than the other, this isn't necessarily true. Give yourselves time to talk about your loss and time to cry together. Be kind to yourself, too. Don't try to be a superhero. If the day is an extremely difficult one, call a special person and tell them you are sad and need to talk and cry. Getting friends and family to listen to your feelings can be a great help. There is comfort in tears. On difficult days, get out of the house and go for a walk or meet someone for a cup of coffee or soft drink.

Your anger, especially anger at God, may surprise you. You may experience feelings that you are being punished for something you have done. No God would ever be so cruel as to take away your child for punishment. Those feelings are all part of the grieving process. I encourage you to write in a journal to express all your feelings, no matter how bitter or hateful or self-pitying they may be. It's a journal for you and no one else has to read it. If lack of sleep, not being able to eat, or else eating constantly are affecting you, then try to do some physical exercise . . . running, walking, tennis swimming or just good workouts.

The intensity of your grief will not always be as painful as it is in the beginning. Don't feel guilty if you can once again laugh at something--hurray for you! When periods of sadness occur further and further apart, you are making progress. If at some point in time you feel stuck in your grief, you may want to find a grief counselor. After all, if your arms were broken you would have a professional mend it and so, too, a professional can help mend a broken heart. If there is a support group in your area, think about becoming a part of the group. It's comforting to talk with people who understand and relate to your loss. It's good to share experiences.

I never held, touched or saw our baby, Mary. I have no memories to look at. However, our lives are richer for having known her in our minds and hearts, even if it was . . . only for a moment. May you find peace in your hearts, too.

Patty

MARTHA EISE IS A COUNSELOR AND COORDINATOR OF A. M. E. N. D. (AIDING MOTHERS AND FATHERS EXPERIENCING NEONATAL DEATH). SHE IS THE MOTHER OF TWO BABIES WHO DIED.

Dear Parents,

I wish I could be with you right now, sharing a cup of coffee or tea. Since this is not possible, I will try to help you the best I can through this letter. I am so sorry to hear of the death of your baby. I can assure you I know what you are feeling. I have been there myself.

You are probably feeling very sad, maybe even angry. You might be feeling that no one really cares or understands how you feel. I can only assure you that you will not always feel as bad as you do now. I want to also tell you that you will never forget your baby, nor will you want to forget. That baby was a very special part of you and you will find yourself wondering, as the years go by, just what that child would look like or be doing. I know, because I do.

You are probably receiving some well-meaning advice from friends and family. "You are young, you can have other children. You can be glad the baby did not live, it would have been harder to lose it later. You have an angel in heaven." I know that none of these things are what you want to hear. Try to remember that people are only trying to make you feel better.

Another thought--please do not put a timetable on your grieving. Give yourself all the time you need. You will find that some days you notice you are feeling better and then you will have some bad days. That's all right, just give yourself time.

I hope this letter will be of some help to you. Please believe me when I say I know how and what you are feeling and I care.

Love and Concern,

Martha

TERRY MORGAN IS PASTOR OF GOOD SHEPHERD LUTHERAN CHURCH, KETTERING, OHIO. HE IS THE AUTHOR OF "TELLING EMILY GOODBYE."

Dear Parents,

SHE WOULD BE TEN NOW . . .
And I wonder, would she have dancing curls and sparkling eyes and a dimple in her cheek like her mother?
SHE WOULD BE TEN NOW . . .
Perhaps too old for laps but not too old to be tucked in at night and kissed and told not to let the bedbugs bite.
SHE WOULD BE TEN NOW . . .
Daddy's little girl, full of ideas and opinions and laughter, like her father.

DEAR
PARENTS
~
A
Collection
of Letters
to
Bereaved
Parents
~
40

We lost her ten years ago. She was our first child. She was our last child. We had awaited her with eager expectation. I had bought a crib and sanded it down myself and repainted it in the garage. We painted the room and it became a child's room with a cute little lamp with clowns on the side. Oh, but that room would never hold a child nor would we. You see, we learned late in Barbara's pregnancy, that our child was afflicted with a severe congenital malformation, a neural tube defect called anencephaly. Children with this malformation, the doctor told us as we sat in stunned silence, are born alive but usually die within a few hours.

We made a lot of mistakes, Dear Parents, but we were on a road without maps and did not know the way:

WE DID NOT NAME HER. We had decided to call our first child, if it was a girl, Emily, a name I had suggested. But when we had this broken child who lived only four hours, we told the nurses just to call her 'Baby Girl' on the certificates that marked her birth and death. We have since given her back her name and mourned her death and celebrated her brief life. NAME YOUR CHILD. It is a real child, the loss a real loss. The birth is a real birth, the death a real death.

WE DID NOT SEE HER. You see, she was badly broken and in our brokenness we did not think we had the strength to look on hers. I have since, as pastor, seen such broken babies. They are not hard to look at nor to hold. I have held them while their parents took pictures. I have watched their mothers hold them as they quietly slipped from this world into the next where God would hold them for eternity.

WE DID NOT TRY TO HAVE OTHER CHILDREN. We learned through genetic counseling that our chances of having another such afflicted baby was 1 in 4 or 5. We felt the risk was too high, the pain of having another such afflicted baby would be too great. Now as we have grown into middle age, we wish we had taken the risk. One woman who wrote to us has had two anencephalic children, but she also had three healthy children. No, the healthy ones will not replace the broken ones; one child cannot replace another. They are as unique as their fingerprints. When folks say to you, "You'll have another," know that subsequent children will never take the place of the child you have lost, but other children will fill a place in your heart--not the lost child's place, but another place waiting to be filled.

IF YOU CANNOT HAVE ANOTHER, know that being a couple without being parents is not fatal. Barbara and I decided we would not let it pull us apart but instead we shared a grief that pulled us much closer together. Suddenly you will notice in the world that there are other couples without children, some by choice but most by chance and you will be drawn to them. You will also be drawn to couples WITH CHILDREN. They will be afraid of you, wondering if it will hurt to bring their children near. Go near them. Go near their children. It does not hurt.

SHE WOULD BE TEN NOW. Not a day goes by that I do not think of her, wonder about her, try to picture her in my mind. Losing a child is not something you will get over, but it is something you will get through and something you can grow through as well as go through. When I think of Emily now and her name is whispered down the corridors of my dreams, it is less often with sorrow and more often with joy . . . joy that someday we will see her in that kingdom where all brokenness will be healed, all tears wiped away and the eternal afternoon of laughter will begin. I see her there now,

AND SHE IS TEN.

Terry

Dear Parents,

If I could spend some time with you, there would be several things we could share. I would like to hear the details of what happened, so I could better understand the many things that add to your pain.

DEAR
PARENTS
~
A
Collection
of Letters
to
Bereaved
Parents
~
42

If your baby died recently you probably feel there is no light at the end of the darkness you now experience. You probably feel that no one understands and you may wonder if most even care. For you, it feels like the whole world has stopped and yet other people go on as if nothing ever happened. There is a real feeling of isolation. So many thoughts and ideas come to mind and they leave as quickly as they came. You feel disoriented and find it difficult to concentrate. It is difficult to remember beyond a few seconds. At times your mind seems cluttered with many thoughts and other times your mind seems blank.

You have many questions: "How do I handle this depressing time? Will I ever get better? I feel so alone--doesn't anyone understand or care? Will I ever be able to think clearly again?"

As crazy as you may feel, know that this is a normal grief response. Once the initial numbness wears off, deep feelings seem to bombard you--feelings you would rather deny. Perhaps you feel anger, perhaps even anger at God. Find ways to express the feelings verbally and sometimes physically. A brisk walk, pounding a soft pillow or a punching bag are healthy ways of expressing anger.

Just as you need to talk out your anger with another person, also talk with God of your feelings and anger directed at God. In a relationship you need to be honest with the other person. God understands our feelings and will not strike us down if we share our anger. You may feel jealous--of others who have children, of those who are pregnant, jealous of those who have no difficulties in pregnancy. Remember that you have not chosen those feelings, they came because you feel violated or feel an injustice was done to you.

Allow yourself to be in touch with your feelings so you can begin to process them. There is a tendency to say that you should not feel this way. If you try to think, feel and act as others say you should and suppress those feelings, it will interfere with your processing the grief and delay healing. Do listen to your feelings and explore them with a listening partner.

Be realistic in the expectations you place on yourselves. Each person grieves differently according to their personality, their past experiences and coping styles. Don't compare yourself with others. Search until you find a listening partner who will let you tell your feelings and experience again and again. Allow yourself time to grieve without setting time limits. Keep the communication with those who are supportive and with your partner. Let others know that you do not expect them to take away your pain, that you do not expect them to have answers, but that you appreciate their being there to listen when you need them. Accept and ask for the comfort you receive from hugs.

When others make disorienting remarks on a different wave length, don't assume that you are wrong. Listen to your heart and trust your feelings. If you doubt yourself, ask someone who understands grief--another grieving parent may be helpful. In response to disorienting statements of others simply say, "I used to feel that way, but since my child has died I feel differently . . ." then express your feelings. Read from the many books and articles now available. The printed word, too, helps validate your experience and feelings.

Writing puts you in touch with deeper feelings and gives perspective as those feelings are seen outside yourself. Write for yourself or others who understand. Listen to music that moves you deeply. Search for supportive people in your area, for mutual-help groups or people with whom you can correspond. Processing grief alone is difficult. There may be a time when it would be helpful to seek professional counseling from a Bereavement Counselor. Grief is normal, yet we know that there are times when it is quite difficult to cope without the aid of someone to guide us through those times.

Having experienced bereavement, and having walked that path with hundreds of families I have come to see that you, too, will come through this painful time if you have support. I believe in the human spirit and the strength and healing that comes from a power greater than ourselves. You are not alone. There are many of us who will support you through this time. We know you are vulnerable and we will be gentle as we walk with you. Peace.

Sister Jane Marie

Sarah Ewing is a retired hospital chaplain. She has co-authored such books as Newborn Death, Miscarriage and was a pioneer in caring for parents.

Dear Parents,

It makes sense that you're hurt when people don't seem to care that your world has just crashed in. Very likely they really do care - they just don't understand. That makes sense, too. Their lives haven't changed like your life has.

Your friends may have been really supportive at first. But now they act as if you ought to be "over it." They may change the subject when you want to talk about your child. They don't know what to say, because they didn't know your child like you did.

DEAR
PARENTS
~
A
Collection
of Letters
to
Bereaved
Parents
~
44

So why don't they just listen? A lot of people have never learned to listen if they don't know what to say back. They'd "fix it" if they could, but they can't so they feel uncomfortable and change the subject or give you advice.

Even your family may act like it's "all over now, and it's time to get on with your life." Maybe they hurt for you more than you think, and they don't know how to "fix it" either. But most of all, it's that their lives haven't changed like yours. They really can't know how yours has changed because they can't get in your heart and feel the pain.

What do you do? Be honest. When they ask, "How are you doing?" you don't have to say, "Fine." Say something like, "It's hard, but I'm coping the best I can." When they say, "Come on, it's been a month now!" you can just say, "I know you can't understand." If they say some of those dumb things people say, just tell them you don't see it that way.

When other people's lives are going right on, they tend to forget yours isn't. If you can, find a support group where you can talk out your feelings with people who do understand. Or find someone who's good at listening--your pastor, a hospital chaplain or social worker. Or maybe you can find another parent who has experienced your kind of grief. God is a good listener. You can be completely honest with Him about your feelings, and He won't change the subject!

Whatever you do, be patient with your feelings. They'll go up and down, with more downs than ups at first. When you quit hurting so terribly, and start to smile again, you'll find you love your child just as much. Death is never the end of loving. St. Paul said, "Faith, hope and love last on forever, and the greatest of these is love."

Faith, hope and love are important in your life right now. You'll make it through! My love to you, too.

Sarah

Marilyn Gryte is the author of several books, including,
No New Baby, for sibling loss.
She currently is a presenter for the American Academy of Bereavement in Arizona.

Dear Parents,

As a nurse I have sometimes been there when your crushing fears were confirmed. There in the hospital, the labor room, the emergency room when the unspeakable words were spoken, "I'm sorry . . . your child is dead." Words that explode a heart.

At those times I wear my own helplessness knowing I cannot ease your pain. I do not tell you, "I know how those words feel." I don't. (Oh, God, may I never--and yet I know, too, may). As a nurse and a counselor, what I offer you in those moments, those hours we spend together is what I have myself. The commitment that I will not flee from your pain. The commitment that I will do all I can to not make your burden more unbearable.

What I ask is for you to sometime-later-tell us who are 'helpers' what we do that helps a little, and what we do that makes it harder. Tell us--honestly, really. You are our teachers. You teach us how to be with those who mourn.

Marilyn

Torn

While morphine eases the pain
of your well-sutured incision,
and replenishing fluid drips
into your vein,
I sit with you, yearning to infuse
a few drops of courage
into your soul,
and to gently touch together
the torn edges of your heart.

Loss

Only storms of tears
and floods of time
can quench the fire of devastation.
And when the blaze is snuffed
down to a smolder,
it is not over, not over.
There is still the whole city
of the heart to rebuild.

Grief

Grief feels like a cave,
an aimless groping
into a black, deepening void.
Into your hand I press
the only candle I have,
a message
to flicker in the darkness of your soul:
Grief feels like a cave, but it
is not a cave.
Grief is a tunnel, a journey.
The blackness is the same.
The only difference is Hope.

MARION COHEN WROTE SHE WAS BORN: SHE DIED, & AN AMBITIOUS SORT OF GRIEF
MARION'S DAUGHTER, KARIN, DIED SHORTLY AFTER BIRTH.

Dear Parents,

What can I say? Or rather--of the many things I WANT to say, what should I choose? I've had an actual cup of coffee (in my case, vegetable soup) with a host of other parents, but then I've mostly listened, I've written to many parents who write to me about my poems, but I respond then to what they write. It's harder to compose this letter to you.

DEAR
PARENTS
~
A
Collection
of Letters
to
Bereaved
Parents
~
46

Perhaps the most comforting thought I can give you--and you'll hear this from others--is that neither your life nor your happiness is over. You will never forget, true, you will never stop loving your child, but the sense of shock, of immediacy, and of pain, will not always be what it is now. Even the sadness, later, will be more pensive than painful.

But later is a long time away, and now is now. And the sometimes-comforting cliche, "Time heals all wounds" also says with frustration that nothing else will heal those wounds . . . all you can do is wait. "I can do my exercises religiously and take my vitamins," reads my diary from that horrible period of my life, "but I can't do a damn thing about time. That has to pass and I have to move alongside it. And be conscious." But MY 'now' did end, and so will yours.

There were things that helped me. Locking myself in a room and being alone, writing, sleeping, napping, having my mother instead of me make the bad-news phone calls, lying in my husband's arms, holding him in mine, remembering together, talking All About It to each other. My sense of humor helped me--or rather, denying myself this humor, which came naturally to me, would have hindered. Making plans, like doing a poetry reading in six months--made me realize that time WAS passing after all.

Teaching one evening a week, answering condolence calls, receiving a few visitors, talking All About It and listening to their totally unrelated problems gave me the dose of perspective. Imagining Kerin alive was often what put me to sleep at night and dreaming of her is probably what gave me the strength to wake up.

It was a full two months before I could say I felt even a wee bit better. It was only then I was able to get anything passing for enjoyment out of things I'd previously enjoyed--thrift-shopping, piano playing, building a snowman with the kids--and I'd be a liar if I omitted sex.

This isn't an advice letter, but if I were to advise there'd be three important points:

1. Don't try to forget, don't not-dwell on it, don't deny and don't deny your grief. Grief is what you have instead of your child and you need at least that.

2. Don't try to avoid ambivalence and contradictions in the months to come, you will encounter many. You'll feel ashamed, you'll feel proud. You'll feel guilty, you'll feel powerless. You'll want to know you're normal, yet you'll have times of wanting you and your child to be special. You'll want time to pass, yet you'll feel time taking you farther and farther away from your child. Let yourself feel what you feel, even if one feeling contradicts another.

3. Try to identify activities that feel helpful to you, that feel most right. Now is the time to be selfish. You are the most important person in the drama. Don't worry about social obligations. I warn you that nothing will be very helpful, and nothing will feel right, not really. Everything will have a nightmarish tint. But as time passes, there will be more and more things that help, fewer things that hurt.

In conclusion, Dear Parent, I'm so sorry. What I wouldn't give to present to you, instead of this letter, your child. If only Dear Parents could be, instead of a collection of letters, a catalog of our children and where to claim them. But for you who are in your now, I wish you the very best possible.

In comraderie and sincerity

Marion

DARCIE SIMS IS V. P., NATIONAL BOARD OF DIRECTORS, THE COMPASSIONATE FRIENDS. SHE IS A GRIEF MANAGEMENT SPECIALIST AND A PSYCHOTHERAPIST. TONY WAS A HOSPITAL ADMINISTRATOR WITH THE U. S. ARMY AND IS DIRECTOR OF BIG A AND COMPANY PUBLISHING. THEIR SON, AUSTIN VAN, DIED OF A RARE FORM OF BRAIN CANCER AT THE AGE OF 13 MONTHS IN 1976.

Dear Parents,

Who are we now that our child is dead? Am I still a mother if there is no child to kiss? Am I still a dad if there is no one to tuck in at night? How can we go on living when our child has died? We feel cheated, betrayed, robbed of our child's presence and our future as well.

Alone, we are angry, confused, hurt, afraid. No words ease your heartache. But with the linking of arms, the clasp of hands, we become a family, welded together by the pain and terror of grief. But this isn't enough. You need each other. The grief has shattered your world. How can your marriage survive?

Each of you will grieve separately and differently. Be patient. Temper expectations of each other with compassion and tolerance. Grief is not a sign or weakness nor a lack of faith. It is the price we pay for love.

Our greatest fear is that, alone, we will turn away from living--that we close our hearts to love, because losing a child hurts so very much. And yet, it is exactly that hurt that begins the healing. It is acknowledging and living that pain that brings forth the energy and strength to allow healing and hope to return.

The intensity of your pain truly does pass. It seems to be replaced by moments of hurt, moments of hot tears, moments of breathlessness . . . but now only moments when once we knew it would last forever! Let the joy of your child's life begin to take the place of the hurt and anger of your child's death.

Recovery from the death of a child is a matter of choice. Time does help heal over open wounds. Scars form and serve as reminders of battles once fought. We learn to live with those scars and slowly they sink into the scheme of our lives. The things we did together, the things we shared, the good times and the bad ones, the funny stories, the holidays, the life we cherished and knew would last forever . . . these are the memories that grief illuminates. One finally comes to know that these things can never be lost. Memories are forever.

Join hands and hearts, not in sadness, but in celebration of the love that brought you together in the first place. We are also linked with you through the love of our son, Austin, the love of your child and of all the children and brothers and sisters who dance across the rainbows ahead of us. We are a family circle, broken by death, mended by love. May love be what you remember most.

With Love,
Darcie and Tony

DEAR PARENTS

~

A Collection of Letters to Bereaved Parents

~

48

DR. WILLIAM (BILL) MILLER IS A WRITER AND PASTORAL COUNSELOR.
HIS SON, KARL ANDREW, DIED WHEN 3 DAYS OLD.

Dear Parents,

I suspect you are wondering how you will ever make it through this loss. You feel and overwhelming load of grief that you wonder if you will be able to survive, or at least maintain your sanity. It is absolutely horrendous. I do not know of any experience that is as wrenching and tearing as the death of your only child.

Death first visited me when I was eight years old. My father just fell over dead of a heart attack. My mother died a year and a half later. I have lost a step-father, a step-mother and a father-in-law to death. But of all these experiences, none has been as profoundly grievous as the death of our son. Nothing in my life has ever caused me to feel so ripped apart as the death of our son.

I remember driving home alone from the hospital the day he died. I remember only because I could not stop sobbing. I remember the burial; I could not stop sobbing there, either. I remember a year later attending the memorial service for the child of friends of ours; Marilyn and I fell apart and went to pieces all over again. We said to each other, "Will we ever get over this?"

No. You don't ever get over it. You don't ever forget. In time you move beyond the pain, yes. In time you come to believe that you will survive and not lose your mind, yes. In time you feel restored and whole again, yes. But you never forget the loss of your child. I think that is good. We can move beyond, but we cannot forget; we do not want to forget. I think that is the way it must be.

It also must be that you wander sometimes aimlessly through the wilderness of anguish before you reach the promised land of peace and healing. It will take time. More time than we like to think. Each of us grievers needs to wrestle with the demons and dragons and despair of crazy thinking before we can begin to feel any kind of restoration and return to a sense of wellness and wholeness. Pay no attention to those who would have you "get it over with" or "pull yourself together" or "get on with your life." Grieve your loss as you must, not as others dictate.
God knows I feel with you in your loss. I want you to believe that the feelings you feel are all normal even though they may frighten you and cause you to think you are losing your mind. In all this, love yourself. Embrace yourself; and if you have a spouse, embrace each other. Share your feelings. Be patient with yourself and each other. And you will slowly move through the valley of the shadows and finally step into the sunlight once again. There are many of us who share in your feelings. And even though you may not know us, believe that we walk with you in spirit, on your journey.

Bill

MARY JOHNSTON-DAVIS IS CO-AUTHOR OF THE ROMANCE NOVEL, LOVE'S LEGACY. SHE HAS EXPERIENCED SEVERAL MISCARRIAGES AND IS UNABLE TO HAVE CHILDREN.

Dear Parents,

You are standing out there in the dark of night, huddled close under your large black umbrella of tears. It is hard to realize now that your total, all-consuming pain will someday diminish. You will recover from the bitter blow that life has dealt you. I can say that because 10 years ago my husband and I were huddled close together under our veil of tears when the doctor told us our child, Amy, was dead.

Amy was the little snowflake that began to dance in my womb in early Fall in Upstate New York as the cold winter winds blew harshly around our little Cape Cod house. We were holding our breath since I was a high-risk patient. We trusted our faith in God. However, during a harsh blizzard, the worst one in history, Amy's tiny feet stopped dancing beneath my ribs. I still remember the sinking feeling when the doctor told me she was dead . . . the shock of telling my husband out in the hall.

My husband was a Lt. in the Air Force. He stayed with me most of the time, leaving to call our parents and tell them the bad news. The head chaplain at the base drove 12 miles through icy roads and blowing snow to be with us. He arrived in his Air Force parka, looking more like a ski teacher than a chaplain. With his sandy blonde hair, he was so kind. I can hear myself saying, "It's God's Will and everything will be all right," smiling through my tears. Inside I was so angry I could not talk to God for a long time.

When you lose a child you lose a dream. One of my favorite sayings is carved on a grave stone in a cemetery babyland. It says, "Step softly . . . a dream lies here."

Amy was not well formed, even for 4 1/2 months. There was a lot of blood and tissue, but I will always cherish the memory of a young nurse who attended me. I never knew her name, but I will always see her fine bronze face and her long dark hair in a neat bun. She was almost six feet tall. As she turned to take the cold steel bed pan away, she gently wrapped a white towel around it . . . and turned at the doorway and asked, hesitantly, "Would you like to see your baby?" It took all my strength to raise up and look at the tiny pieces that made up our dream. In her wisdom I think she sensed I would never carry a child to that point again. She laughed softly and said, "She sure was long and thin and I think her feet were the longest part of her." That comforted me. My big feet had long been a joke in our family. What touched me was when the nurse said, "Your baby."

DEAR
PARENTS
~
A
Collection
of Letters
to
Bereaved
Parents
~
50

We left the hospital the next day despite the blizzard and came home to a dark, empty house, our arms aching, even our cat, Moses, was aware of the loss.

The snows of our harsh winter finally melted in late March, but it was winter in my heart for a long time. Looking back over the 10 years of our journey down grief's sometimes winding and twisting path, I can see the stages we went through for healing. The biggest step was joining a support group for parents.

Our grief has come full circle. I know it's hard for you to think of enduring life without your child, but somewhere inside you will find an inner strength to face the dawn of each new day. Time is a friend! I can talk about Amy now, but that came after 7 years of ups and downs.

I attended a workshop with Joy and Marv Johnson, the most wonderful caring people I have ever met. Marv asked how many of us had written poems or letters to our dead child. I shyly raised my hand. His next question blew my mind. He asked, "How many of you have had your dead child write back to you?"

"Why not?" I thought. And about two weeks later I sat down and wrote to Amy and asked her to write back. A few days later she did. Sitting with a sheet of blue paper, the words came from deep inside me, but they were Amy's words and such a comfort. I urge you to use your pen as a tool for healing or a tape recorder to keep a journal to air your feelings.

Good night, and as you sleep may the wings of dawn rise up to meet you and restore your body and soul . . . strong once more to face the world.

Mary

SHEROKEE ISLE WROTE EMPTY ARMS AND CO-AUTHORED **MISCARRIAGE: A SHATTERED DREAM.**
HER BRENNAN DIED AT BIRTH. MARAMA MISCARRIED, AND SHEROKEE ALSO HAD A
MISCARRIAGE DUE TO AN ECTOPIC PREGNANCY. SHE FOUNDED THE PREGNANCY AND
INFANT LOSS CENTER IN MINNESOTA AND IS THE MOTHER OF KELLAN AND TREVOR.

Dear Parents,

I am so sorry your child has died. How unfair, how unjust! No matter how old
your child, whether your child was miscarried, stillborn, died as an infant or older
or even adult child . . . I extend my hand, my heart and my soul to you. I too, have
walked down a similar path.

DEAR
PARENTS
~
A
Collection
of Letters
to
Bereaved
Parents
~
52

Many people are likely to support you during the first few weeks while you are in
shock, when you feel crazy, isolated and possibly quite confused. When you begin
to wake up from what you hope is a 'nightmare' you may find little support and
understanding. That is when I'd especially like to visit with you.

What words of advice, what comfort can I offer? I know I can't take your pain
away. No one can. The long, lonely struggle of grief and mourning must be done
by you. But you need not be alone. As I touch you and sit with you, I offer my listening ear. You need a chance to talk about your child, your dreams, hopes and
aspirations. What is lost now that your child has gone? What do you have to hold
on to?

The importance of memories is one thing I would remind you of. Whenever anyone
dies we dearly cherish the memories we have, even the painful ones. Those memories are all we have left. Don't be afraid to sit with them, to wallow in them and to
remember with all your heart. That is a healthy process which aids us in putting
their lives and death in perspective.

Seek support. Which of your friends and family and co-workers can really listen and
let you cry, scream, lament, wallow or whatever you need to do?

If you have a partner, try to understand your mate's pain, yet don't try to match it.
You will each be on different time tables, have separate needs and possibly unique
perspectives on how to 'recover' from this. Rather than letting your differences separate you, use them to work together, realizing you need not mourn or grieve over
your child in the same way.

You both loved and still love this child. One mother said she was having trouble believing her husband really cared for their daughter who was miscarried. She was able to understand when she looked at her family and realized they coped with wounds and crises in a different way than hers. When someone in their family had a wound, they said, "Let it alone, don't pick it and it will get better on its own."

She believed if there was a wound it needed to be drained (picked at, talked about) in order to heal. While she was draining her pain, her husband was letting it be and waiting for it to subside. The difference could easily have become a stumbling block for them if they had not figured out why they were different.

Don't be hard on yourself. While others may put pressure on you to get over this, move on and quit lamenting, remember you, too, might be putting pressure on yourself. Don't be afraid of wallowing, mourning, experiencing the feelings. It is when you get those feelings out, do the grief work that is part of loving and losing, that you find in time you are feeling better. The more you fight the feelings, stuff the feelings and hope they go away, the longer they will be there, waiting to overwhelm you.

When I wrote **Empty Arms** after Brennan died, I wallowed in my grief and dwelled on it every day for months and months. Still, years later I talk about it quite frequently. In those early months and years the energy I used to think, talk, cry, scream and write was well worth the health I have recovered since. Although I never want to totally lose my emotion and tears for my babies, I can say I don't feel the need to shed many now. I have worked through it and with it to a place where I have found much more joy and satisfaction than tears and heartache. I wish that for you someday.

You are not alone in your loss and heartache. Please know that others like myself have been there, too. We care and we will hold your hand and offer guidance when you are ready. You will need to do the hard work of mourning your loss, expressing your feelings and putting this in perspective in your life as you seek your 'new normal.'

My prayers and best wished,

Sherokee

Dear Bereaved Father,

I am very sorry about the death of your child. When my son died, I remember thinking there are no words to describe the myriad of powerful feelings. I have also learned that there are no words I can share to take the pain away or give meaning to your sense of loss. The truth is, the future will be forever different and your grief . . . well . . . will be with you forever, though I believe eventually you'll learn to live with it. And you will learn to go on living.

What advice do I have? First, attend to your grief! Someone wrote, "The pain that is unavailable cannot be healed." After my initial outpouring of grief, I felt I needed to be strong for my wife. I buried my son in the ground and buried myself in busy-ness. I discovered much later that my wife concluded I didn't really care about my son. I did not listen to the chaplain's advice. He said, "who said you had to be strong to be supportive, go have a good cry on each other's shoulders." I discovered that grief is one of those "pay me now or pay me later" realities. Let the tears flow. Seek a healthy outlet for your anger. Share your feelings of guilt. Give your sense of helplessness and depression time and space.

Mothers and fathers grieve differently. Her grief is not better or worse, just different. Her coping style is different. Be patient with her AND yourself. Grief is a roller-coaster of emotions. You will not ride the ups and downs at the same time. You cannot take her grief away, but you can share it. You cannot prevent her from suffering, but you can prevent her from suffering for the wrong reasons. Be a loving listener. Share your feelings. Hold each other tenderly and often.

Men often have trouble reaching out for support. Certainly many have trouble offering support to men. I got so tired of hearing, "How's your wife doing?" I rarely heard, "How are YOU doing?" I cannot stress how important I believe it is for you to find and use one or more support persons. No one can do your grieving for you; no one grieves alone! I urge both of you to join a bereaved parent support group. Consider reading together a book about grief.

I'd like to share a few practical tips. Try to get some exercise. Walking may be good for your mind and your body. Resist the temptation to over-work; pace yourself carefully. If you have lost your appetite, be attentive to maintaining a high level of fluid intake. Avoid coping by the use or abuse of alcohol or drugs.

Your child has died. Your dreams and memories will never die. Death demands that you let go though that is no easy process. Letting go is not forgetting. Letting go is ultimately forgiving this tragedy, experiencing acceptance along with the sadness and having the courage to risk loving again and again. I wish you a healthy journey through your grief, from another bereaved father.

Jim

DEAR
PARENTS
~
*A
Collection
of Letters
to
Bereaved
Parents*
~
54

Sisters and Brothers

We are often shuttled off to friends and left out of our family.

I know you do this to protect us from painful feelings, but please . . .

let us be a part of our family!

ALLIE SIMS

SARAH BLACKBURN IS 11. HER BROTHER, DJ, DIED OF CANCER.
SHE IS PART OF THE FAMILY OF **TIMOTHY DUCK,** AND HER MOTHER, LYNN,
MENTIONS SARAH IN HER LETTER.

Dear Parents,

You may think that a young child is not affected much by death. In fact, we may be affected by death more than you think. I was nine when my brother died. He had a friend who was only six when he died. She cried almost as much as I did. We still think about him a lot. Now I'm 11 and she is 8. When you think about it you may notice that we weren't much older than he was, so we understand how much pain he went through.

Now that I am eleven and in sixth grade, I hate it when people talk about my brother when I'm around and then apologize for it. I like it when they talk about my brother. It re-lives the memories of good and bad times. Another thing I hate is when someone close to you dies and you act like you don't care. It makes it worse. I wish I could talk to the people who act like that. It's not going to make it better. It's probably not what you would want someone to do over yourself. My brother may be dead, but we learned to accept and deal with it. We still go to Christmas parties and see friends, nurses and doctors that we won't forget.

Sometimes I didn't want to go near him. But he doesn't haunt me because I didn't. The thing I'm trying to say is, don't hold in all your feelings no matter how old you are. It's just better to let them out and deal with them. I may still be young, but I still understand people.

P. S. This was also written for all the young children who have to deal with death.

Sarah

DEAR
PARENTS
~
*A
Collection
of Letters
to
Bereaved
Parents*
~
56

ALICIA (ALLIE) SIMS IS THE AUTHOR OF **AM I STILL A SISTER?** A BOOK WRITTEN TO BEREAVED SISTERS AND BROTHERS IN SEARCH OF THEIR OWN IDENTITIES AFTER THE DEATH OF A SIBLING.

Dear Parents,

My name is Allie Sims and my brother, Austin, died when I was 4. A lot of people thought I was too young to know what was going on or to grieve very much. But they were wrong! Children DO grieve. Sometimes, adults are too wrapped up in their own grief to realize that we hurt, too. We are often shuttled off to friends and relatives and left out of our family. I know you do this to protect us from painful feelings and experiences, but please . . . let us be a part of our family. We need to be surrounded by the love and comfort of Mom and Dad. Even if you don't feel very comforting, you are!

Please don't shut us out! I'm as lost and confused as you are. We need each other, now more than ever. You are afraid to be weak and cry in front of us. We are afraid to say anything that might upset you. And so, in our silence, in our slammed doors and closed hearts, we hurt and ache . . . alone. Why are we locked in fear that destroys communications, fear that burns bridges, fear that seems to take up residence in our homes?

Where is my family that used to be? In our attempts to protect each other, we miss each other. We see each other, but we cannot find the hands or the hearts to match. Must I lose not only the love of my brother or sister, but your love as well?

It seems hopeless. I want to understand you and I can't. You want me to understand and we're both afraid. It seems easier and safer to stop trying. We turn away . . . taking with us our hurts and sorrows to seek comfort somewhere else because our family no longer seems safe and secure.

I cannot live with the ghost you have created. I cannot become my brother. I cannot live our your dreams for him. I have my own shoes to wear, my own path to follow. Please let me be me as we learn to dance together again.

We are still a family and silence only hurts.

I love you and I want us to work through this together. It's the only way for us to survive. Please don't shut me out. Let's reach our to each other, across our pain and grief to share a hug.

Thank you for listening. May you hear your own children as well.

Allie

SARA KUSHNICK IS THE TWIN OF SAM, WHO WAS ONE OF THE FIRST CHILDREN
IN THE U. S. DIAGNOSED WITH AIDS, CONTRACTED FROM BLOOD TRANSFUSIONS
GIVEN HIM AS AN INTENSIVE CARE INFANT.
THE KUSHNICKS WERE FEATURED IN A PEOPLE MAGAZINE ARTICLE IN 1984.

Dear Parents,

My brother Sam was only three years old when he died. Sometimes it's hard to
remember. Sam was one minute older than me, but one day he stopped growing
and I was so much taller than him.

DEAR
PARENTS
~
A
Collection
of Letters
to
Bereaved
Parents
~
58

I remember when my brother used to have to take all these pills and crummy stuff.
It didn't feel really good to have a brother who was always feeling bad and didn't
like to do a lot of things.

Finally, one day they did a test and said that Sam was very sick--he had AIDS and
there wasn't a cure. There was nothing they could do.

When Sam died, I felt all confused. I really didn't know what was going to happen.
All the time I asked Mommy and Daddy, "What's going to happen?" and they would
talk to me.

Then I got kicked out of nursery school. They said that I had AIDS too, but I didn't.
If I had AIDS, I wouldn't be there. Some of the children's mothers said, Don't play
with Sara, she has AIDS. Don't they know AIDS isn't like the chicken pox or flu? I
kissed my brother and I hugged my brother, and I don't have AIDS. It doesn't feel
very good, but I forget all about all of that stuff.

Sometimes when I look at pictures of Sam, I cry, especially the pictures of his last
birthday party when we were three. Mom and Dad are right there. Now, I have a
perfect life and you know, everything is fine. I still miss my brother a whole lot.
And Mom and Dad are still fighting for a cure for AIDS. It feels sort of weird when
you think about it. Look at all those other people who died of AIDS and all the sadness. That's really all I have to say.

Sara Rose Kushnick

DENISE CARLSON IS PAULA'S DAUGHTER. HER OLDER SISTER, DEANNE, DIED AT AGE 16.

Dear Parents,

My sister, Deanne was in a tragic car accident in May. A week later, on Mother's Day, Deanne died a brain death. When Deanne died, it felt like I died, too! What I find helps me cope is:

Talking to my Mom and Dad.
Writing down how I feel.
Crying as much as I want.

My dog and cat seem to help me cope with some bad days. I can tell my animals anything and everything I feel, and I know they will always keep it private! There isn't a replacement for Deanne, but it is always nice to have my animals and family.

When I first found out that Deanne had died, I couldn't think of any reason why life should go on. But I realize now, 2 years later, that time does not stand still; although it took me a year and a half to realize it. Time can be your worst enemy or it can be your best friend. It's what you make of it that counts.

Time is still the age-old medicine. It heals in measured doses, slowly, surely.

But often you cannot see through the pain to the new horizons. Time is on your side, and it not only heals and helps with the grieving process, but also gives new strength and creativity. The most creative, beautiful work can be the result of a grieving soul. Your loss is deep and painful, but the new horizons opened to you can, and will, bring a new respectful, joyous look at life. The flower of your soul is just starting to bloom into a new beginning. Have faith in yourself as there truly is an inner strength you can draw on.

Denise

WHEN ROBERT KENNEDY'S FUNERAL TRAIN TRAVELED ACROSS THE COUNTRY, MILLIONS OF PEOPLE STOOD WITH SMALL AMERICAN FLAGS, THEIR HATS REMOVED, BLACK ARMBANDS, CRYING OPENLY. OLDER AMERICANS HAD LOST A SON . . . YOUNGER ONES A BROTHER. SENATOR EDWARD KENNEDY GAVE US THE EULOGY HE PRESENTED AT BOBBY'S FUNERAL, JUNE 8, 1968. SOMETIMES WE GRIEVE AS A NATION. SENATOR KENNEDY ALSO GRIEVED AS A SIBLING. THE EULOGY ESPECIALLY FITS PARENTS WHOSE CHILD'S DEATH URGES THEM ON TO A CAUSE, AN EFFORT TO FIND MEANING THROUGH ACTION.

Dear Parents,

DEAR
PARENTS
~
A
Collection
of Letters
to
Bereaved
Parents
~
60

When offering condolences to people who have suffered the loss of a loved one, I often say that I, too, know the pain of such a loss, but that in time, one remembers more the wonderful life and love that is shared, rather than the sad time at the end. I share with you words from my brother's eulogy.

"Love is not an easy feeling to put into words. Nor is loyalty, or trust or joy. But he was all of these. He loved life completely and lived it intensely. A few years back, Bobby wrote some words about his own father, and they express the way we feel about him. 'What it really all adds up to is love--not love as it is described with such facility in popular magazines, but the kind of love that is affection and respect, order, encouragement and support. Our awareness of this was an incalculable source of strength, and because real love is something unselfish and involves sacrifice and giving, we could not help but profit from it.'

A speech he made to the young people of South Africa on their Day of Affirmation in 1966 sums up best what he stood for:

'There is discrimination in this world . . . there are differing evils . . . . They reflect the imperfection of human justice, the inadequacy of human compassion, our lack of sensibility toward the sufferings of our fellows.

But we can remember that those who live with us are our brothers, that they share with us the same short moment of life; that they seek – as we do – nothing but the chance to live out their purpose and happiness, winning what satisfaction and fulfillment they can.

Surely this bond of common faith, this bond of common goal, can begin to teach us something. We can learn to look at those around us as fellow men. We can begin to work a little harder to bind up the wounds among us and to become in our own hearts brothers and countrymen once again.

Our answer is to rely on youth--not a time of life but a state of mind, a temper of the will, a quality of imagination, a predominance of courage over timidity, the appetite for adventure over the love of ease. Some believe there is nothing one man or one woman can do against the enormous array of the world's ills. Yet many of the world's great movements, of thought and action, have flowed from the work of a single person.'

'Few of us will have the greatness to bend history itself, but each of us can work to change a small portion of events, and in the total of all those acts will be written the history of this generation. Like it or not, we live in times of danger and uncertainty. The future does not belong to those who are content with today, apathetic toward common problems and their fellow man alike, timid and fearful in the face of new ideas and bold projects. Rather, it will belong to those who can blend vision, reason and courage in a personal commitment to ideals and greatness.

Our future may lie beyond our vision, but it is not completely beyond our control. There is pride in that, even arrogance, but there is also experience and truth. In any event, it is the only way we can live.

This is the way he lived. My brother need not be idealized, or enlarged in death beyond what he was in life, to be remembered simply as a good and decent man, who saw wrong and tried to right it, saw suffering and tried to heal it, saw war and tried to stop it.

Those of us who loved him and who take him to his rest today, pray that what he was to us and what he wished for others will some day come to pass for all the world.

As he said many times, in many parts of this nation, to those he touched and who sought to touch him:

> "Some men see things as they are and say why.
> I dream things that never were and say why not."

Edward

From Caring Others

**DEAR
PARENTS**

~

*A
Collection
of Letters
to
Bereaved
Parents*

~

62

I can't say anything that will make things better,

but I can be there with you and share the anger,

the pain, the bewilderment.

Most of all, I can let you know that I care

and that I won't abandon you.

DR. RUTH HITCHCOCK

ELISABTH KUBLER-ROSS, AUTHOR OF **ON DEATH AND DYING** AND MANY OTHER BOOKS, IS THE GRAND LADY WHO BEGAN THE STUDY OF DEATH AND DYING, RECOGNIZED THE FEELINGS ACCOMPANYING GRIEF, AND OPENED THE WINDOWS OF KNOWLEDGE TO US. ALL THE GREAT CHANGES IN OUR AWARENESS EVENTUALLY LEAD BACK TO HER.

My Dearest . . .

I am so very, very sorry about the death of your child. Your pain and despair have been old and familiar songs to me, songs so well remembered. And because I can remember so clearly, I can also tell you with complete certainty that the joy will come to you again, though it may seem impossible to you now. You will be able to look back and see the face, the funny little mannerisms, the way the hair fell when it was brushed; you will be able to hear the laughter and hold your child close without feeling as if your heart is breaking.

But this change comes ever so slowly, almost imperceptibly. And sometimes the time between now and then is so hard to endure. Your faith in life and happiness and the future may often waver, but grab onto life and anyone and anything that you need for help!

You don't have to be strong or logical or sensible, or any of the things you think you have to be. For me, it turned out to be better when I didn't try to fight the pain but let it roll over me like a giant tidal wave and carry me along with it, until it spent its fury and dropped me gasping but alive on the shores of sanity. And, like any storm, it gradually died. The waves crashed farther and farther apart, and somewhere, without my being aware of it, life became worth living again.

My dear friend, I am a strong swimmer. So when you find yourself being swallowed up in the backwash, close your eyes and feel my arms around you holding you up, and feel my love, one human being to another, one mother's love to another, reaching out across the continent to hold your heart in warmth and comfort while it heals.

Everyday my prayers will be for your pain to ease and for peace to come to you. You know that we are always given what we need, whether we want it or not. You will be given. Just keep right on reaching for it. It is there. My thoughts are ever with you, and my love is flowing to you.

Elisabeth

RUTH HITCHCOCK IS AN ASSISTANT PROFESSOR OF COUNSELING AT WITCHITA STATE UNIVERSITY.

Dear Parents,

Friends have died, aunts, uncles, grandparents have died, my mother died. I have wept and raged and grown numb and wept again. As a counselor, I have worked with children and adults, trying to help them deal with death. Neither personal experience nor professional skills are much help when a child dies, no matter whether that child is an infant or an adult.

DEAR
PARENTS
~
A
Collection
of Letters
to
Bereaved
Parents
~
64

Somewhere, somehow, we have the idea that children aren't supposed to die. Children aren't supposed to hurt in ways that cannot be kissed and hugged away. Parents shouldn't feel hopeless and helpless, and above all, parents aren't supposed to outlive their children. But children do die before parents, and often in pain. Then the world becomes a place that makes less sense than before.

As a counselor, I want to say something brilliant, something that will make the waiting less agonizing, or the suddenness less shattering, or the grieving less painful. I have yet to find words that can do any of those things. Your life has changed and no matter what is said or done, neither you nor your family can be the same. Ever. Yet, as one who has grieved and still grieves, I know that most of the time, there are things that help.

It helps to know that someone is there. It helps to be touched. It helps to know the roller coaster of feelings doesn't mean you're crazy. It helps to have someone who doesn't try to cajole you out of your sadness or shame you out of your anger. It helps to know that little, seemingly uneventful things - a picture, a song, a special day - can send you into a tailspin. It helps to know there is no schedule for dying or grieving. You grieve your own way and in your own time.

I can't say anything that will make things better, but I can be there with you and share the anger, the pain, the bewilderment. Most of all, I can let you know that I care and that I won't abandon you.

Ruth

DEAN KOONTZ, ONE OF THE BEST-KNOWN MYSTERY WRITERS OF OUR DAY, WANTED TO DO A LETTER FOR US AND HE WROTE, "THE BEST LAID PLANS OF MEN BEING EVEN MORE TENUOUS THAN THOSE OF MICE. I'VE NOT FOUND SURCEASE FROM MY WORK. HOWEVER--" AND HE PERMITTED US TO EXCERPT PARTS OF TWILIGHT OF THE DAWN, ONE OF DEAN'S SHORT STORIES APPEARING IN THE BOOK, NIGHT VISIONS 4.

Peter Fallon is an atheist; a practicing, unrelenting, obsessed atheist. His son, Benny, age 8, was raised in a stricter belief system than most religious children. Peter's fight against religion wrestled Santa Claus away from Benny. But when Benny's mother, Ellen, was killed in an accident, Benny stood by the belief that, "She just couldn't NOT be. She's somewhere." When Benny was 10, Peter receives another blow. Benny is dying of cancer:

"'Daddy, I'm scared,' Benny says just before he dies. 'I'm not scared . . . for me. I'm afraid . . . for you. I want us all . . . to be together again . . . like we were before Mommy died . . . but I'm afraid that you . . . won't . . . find us. If you don't believe you can find us . . . then maybe you won't find us.'

'It's all right, Benny,' I said soothingly. I kissed him on the forehead, on his left cheek, and I put my face against his and held him as best I could, trying to compensate with affection for the promise of faith I refused to give.

'Daddy . . . just look for us . . .'

The grey rain streamed down the gray window.
He died while I held him."

Peter, quite wealthy, becomes a wanderer, until . . . a year later, he goes home and stands under the cherry trees where he and Benny had talked together, he and Ellen had loved together, and where Benny had spent his last happy moments.

"Benny had been dead almost nine months, but the trees he had loved were still thriving, and in some way I could not quite grasp, their continued existence meant that at least a part of Benny was still alive. I struggled to understand that crazy idea--and suddenly the cherry blossoms fell. Not just a few. Not just hundreds. Within one minute every blossom on both trees dropped to the ground. Whirling white flowers were as thick as snowflakes in a blizzard. I had never seen anything like it.

I sensed that Benny was not within the tree, that this phenomenon did not conform to pagan belief any more than it did to traditional Christianity. But he was somewhere. He was not gone forever. He was out there somewhere, and when my time came to go where he and Ellen had gone, I only needed to believe that they could be found, and I would surely find them."

Dean

JOSEPH WAMBAUGH IS ONE OF AMERICA'S GREAT MYSTERY WRITERS. HIS COP STORIES CAN BE FOUND IN ANY BOOKSTORE. WE ASKED JOE IF WE COULD USE SOME OF HIS WORDS OF A FATHER'S GRIEF FROM THE SECRETS OF HARRY BRIGHT, A BOOK WHOSE TWO MAIN CHARACTERS ARE GRIEVING FATHERS. HERE, VICTOR WATSON, ONE FATHER, TALKS WITH DETECTIVE SIDNEY BLACKBURN, THE OTHER FATHER. "I CAN'T SAY IT BETTER THAN I SAID IT HERE," JOE TOLD US.

"'Tell me, do you know about depression and despair?' Without waiting for an answer, VictorWatson said, 'I can tell you that despair is not merely acute depression. Despair is MORE than the sum of many terrible parts. Depression is purgatory. Despair is hell.'

DEAR
PARENTS

~

A
Collection
of Letters
to
Bereaved
Parents

~

66

The detective almost sent the Ming-dynasty figurine spinning off the cocktail table, he snatched at the Johnnie Walker so quickly.

Victor Watson didn't notice. He just kept talking in a monotone that was getting spooky. 'Do you know how a man feels when he lost his son? He feels . . . incomplete. Nothing in the whole world looks the same or IS the same. He goes around looking for pieces of himself. Incomplete. And . . . and then all his daydreams and fantasies go back to June of last year. Whatever he's thinking about, it's got to precede the the time he got the phone call about his son. You see, he just keeps trying to turn the clock back. He wants just one more chance. For what? He can't even say for sure. He wants to communicate. What? He isn't sure.' And then Victor Watson breathed a sigh and said: 'The ancient inherited shame of fathers and sons.'

He isn't able to answer his phone at first, the father of a dead boy. Especially since so many people think they have to call to express condolences. One friend calls four times and finally you speak to him and he says, 'Why didn't you return my calls? I want to SHARE your grief.' And you say to him, 'You dumb son-of-a-bitch. if you could share any part of it, I'd give it to you! I'd give it ALL to you, you stupid bastard!' And then of course I lost that friend.

Then for several weeks, all I could think about were the bad moments. I couldn't remember the good times, the good things we had together, Jack and me. Only the problems. You know something? Booze used to make me silly and happy. Now I hardly touch it because it makes me morose and mean.'

'I don't . . . .'

'Listen to me, please,' Victor Watson said. 'I'll share a secret with you. I hope it helps. Sometimes, Sidney, sometimes the father of a dead son has to be careful not to turn the awful outrage AGAINST the boy. Sometimes he might come to feel that the son failed in his OBLIGATION to survive the father. Don't confuse your torment with mine, Sidney. My son didn't fail me!"

Joseph

TRUE FRIENDS . . .
WHEN LIFE GROWS TOUGH, THEY'RE WILLING TO LISTEN

ERMA BOMBECK

For more than 40 years, I have had the best friend you could ever have.

When I told my best friend I was fat, she never said, "I just lost three pounds without even trying."

When we went to a sock hop together in college and she was offered a ride home, she never ditched me.

When I gave myself a home permanent and left the solution on too long, she was the only one to sit with me in the bathroom until my hair grew out.

When I told my best friend my husband gave me two snow tires for my anniversary, she never said, "You should be happy to be remembered."

When I was pregnant and my stomach looked like a tray on a car door in a drive-in, she never said, "There's a glow about pregnant women."

When I had a miscarriage and everyone else in the world said, "There will be other babies," she cried with me over the one I lost.

When she told me she was staying home for the summer, I wouldn't have dreamed of sending her a card from Spain telling her what a great time I was having.

When her mixer broke down, I never asked her if she had sent in the warranty card so she would be covered.

When I moved 3,000 miles away, she never once told me what I was doing to her.

When her mother died, I never said, "She had a rich, full life and she was in her 70's."

When I argued with my husband and begged her for advice, she kept her mouth shut. She just listened.

When we couldn't get a babysitter and I had to bring the kids along to her house for dinner, she never fell apart.

When I had my first autographing party and no one showed up, she never once suggested, "They probably didn't see the ad."

When her political candidate lost and mine won, I never said, "Ha, ha, I told you so."

Every time we got together, neither of us had to say, "I'm glad to see you."

When she was up to her armpits in snow, I never called her to say, "The sun is shining here."

Recently, my best friend lost her child. He was her youngest and was in his 20's. I listened to her, I cried with her. I felt pain that I had never known I could feel. But not once did I say to her, "I know how you feel."

Erma

RABBI EARL GROLLMAN HAS WRITTEN SEVERAL EXCELLENT BOOKS ON GRIEF. TWO WE HIGHLY RECOMMEND ARE **TALKING ABOUT DEATH,** AND **STRAIGHT TALK ABOUT DEATH FOR TEENAGERS.**

Dear Parents,

When you face the death of your child or of anyone you love, remember:

Accept your grief. Expect the physical and emotional consequences of the death of your loved one. Grief is the price you pay for love.

Express your feelings. Don't mask your despair. Cry when you have to; laugh when you can.

Be patient with yourself. Your mind and body and soul need time and energy to mend. Grief is like weeding a flower bed in the summer. You may have to do it over and over again until the seasons change.

Monitor your health. Eat as well as you can. You need nourishment for the physically gruelling experience of grief. Depression can also be lightened by biochemical changes through proper exercise. Put balance back into your life with work and relaxation. Have a complete checkup. Tell the doctor of your loss.

Avoid the abuse of alcohol and drugs. These can sedate for the moment but ultimately can leave the nervous system in shreds. Altering the process of grief work, drugs can conceal legitimate emotions and create problems.

Share the pain of your darkness with a friend or friends. Don't withdraw from others. By your silence, you deny them the opportunity to share yourself. Said Ralph Waldo Emerson, "A friend is a person with whom I may be sincere."

Join a group of others who are grieving. Learning about the experiences of others can offer invaluable insights into your own feelings with support, encouragement and friendship.

DEAR
PARENTS
~
A
Collection
of Letters
to
Bereaved
Parents
~
68

You might seek solace from your religious faith. Even if you ask, How could God allow this to happen? Sorrow can be a spiritual pilgrimage. Religion is something you may wish to use--not lose--during your bereavement with a wisdom that has nourished souls of humankind for untold generations. Just remember that grieving intensely is no more an indication of a weak faith than grieving deeply is proof of a strong faith.

Help others. By devoting your energies to people and causes, you learn to better relate to others, face reality, become more independent and let go of the past by living in the present. "Only the soul that knows the mighty grief can know the mighty rapture." --Edwin Markham

Do what has to be done but delay major decisions. Begin with little things--a single chore that has to be accomplished. That can help restore your confidence. But wait (if you can) before deciding to immediately sell your house or change jobs. Thomas Carlyle said, "Our main business is not to see what lies dimly at a distance but to do what lies clearly at hand."

Determine to live again. Readjustment does not come overnight. Make a start to put the stars back into your sky. Hold on to the hope and keep trying. Resolve to survive each new day and do your best. Know that our good wishes go with you.

Earl

Dear Parents,

I am humbled by the invitation to share in these Coffee Cup Letters, especially since I have not lost a child. But I did not add, "thank God" to that. I don't believe God chose for your child to die or for mine to live. I believe God wills all our children full and abundant lives and that His heart was broken along with yours.

Having stood with families when a loved one has been killed for nearly five years now, I am aware that some of your painful moments have been those in which someone was trying to help and didn't know how. Most of those hurtful sayings come from people who think they are helping, even if they aren't.

"I know how you feel" is usually an effort to share in your suffering, even though to you it feels like a discount of your pain.

"It must have been God's will," may mean that this is the only way they could cope if it happened to them. To you it may be ludicrous to think that of your God.

"He's in a better place," "She doesn't have to suffer now," "It could have been worse . . ." are feeble attempts to try to make it better for you, from those who don't understand you need them to join in your suffering, not make you feel better. "At least you have other children," may be a way of encouraging you to focus on what you have rather than what is gone, not realizing it sounds like you should forget the child who died.

Failing to use your child's name is usually a conscious choice out of the mistaken belief that you can forget your child if she isn't mentioned. They can't imagine themselves in your shoes long enough to realize you will never forget your child and will celebrate every mention of the child's name.

So, how can you respond? Don't gloss it over, because to do so would not be living with honesty and integrity about your feelings. On the other hand, try not to respond out of the rage you may feel. Understand the people who hurt you are almost always trying to help. Try something like:

"You can't possibly know how I feel, but I do appreciate your willingness to try to share my pain." "No, I don't believe this was God's will. I believe He loves us and stands with us in our suffering." "Thanks for trying to help, and someday I may decide I agree with you, but that's not my experience right now."

It will take time, patience, and even practice to figure out which responses feel right for you. And it's a shame you have to exert energy in that way when you feel your very life is slipping away. But as you do, you will be planting seeds which may enable other grievers of the future to suffer a little less from those who mean well but don't think enough before they speak.

Janice

DEAR
PARENTS

~

*A
Collection
of Letters
to
Bereaved
Parents*

~

70

KAREN WILSON IS AN ONCOLOGY NURSE IN A CHILDREN'S HOSPITAL.
HER LETTER IS TO TWO PARENTS WHO SHARED AN IMPORTANT PART OF LIFE WITH HER.

Dear Stan and Paula,

It's been 3 weeks since Jason died and I can't get him off my mind. As I write my pain floods back and I need to talk about him--as I know you do, too. We've been through so much together. The day he was diagnosed 5 years ago seems like yesterday. Even then, he made sure everyone told him exactly what they were doing and even when we had to hurt him he tried so hard not to move.

Leukemia is such an ugly word. It conjures up all the images of bone marrow tests, hair loss, vomiting, etc.! But is also reminds me of courage, trust and love. We all knew from he beginning we'd have to grit our teeth, do the painful stuff then get on with the hugs, kisses, prizes and special trips to brighten Jason's life.

Three years of treatment seemed like an eternity but then, all of a sudden, it was over! I'll never forget the off-therapy party you held. Then, 2 years later, when you called, worried about some bruising, I reassured you. His blood counts looked good, and every kid bruises when they play hard. But the bruising didn't stop. The enemy was back. There were a lot of tears that day, but Jason, true to form, said, "Don't worry, Karen. Everything will be all right."

When I worked with Jason here at the hospital, we talked about being sick and how he hated it. We would tell stories and he would wonder what it was like in Heaven. He was only 9, but far wiser than his years. As he became sicker and sicker, he told me he was afraid he might die. He was so worried about his mom, dad, brother and sister. He didn't want you to be so sad. He knew he was loved.

The day he died he told me he knew this was going to be the day. When he slipped into a coma we all kept vigil and when he woke up and said, "I see Jesus," we didn't know what to think. The smile on his face was radiant and it was obvious he was able to see something we couldn't. Within an hour he was gone. Our special little guy had fought the good fight and was at peace. His spirit is still very much with us. I don't think I'll ever be able to see a T-bird car without thinking of him and his collection.

I needed to write this so I could put my feelings on paper. You two are wonderful people and I will always appreciate the asset you've been to my life. I'm a better person for having loved him and you, even though it did hurt sometimes.

My love to you. I hope to see you soon. Remember, as you heal, there will be good days and bad days. You'll think you're losing your mind. You're not. Talking helps--to each other and to other parents who have lost a child. Keeping a diary helps, too. By reading what you have written 6 months before, you'll realize the progress though it seems like you're going nowhere. God bless your days ahead. I'll be praying for sunshine and smiles.

Karen

JIM CAMPBELL THE AUTHOR OF **SECRET PLACES,** A BOOK FOR CHILDREN WHO HAVE A PARENT DIE. HE HAS ALSO CONTRIBUTED TO MANY OTHER BOOKS PUBLISHED BY THE CENTERING CORPORATION. HE CURRENTLY LIVES IN ALASKA.

DEAR
PARENTS

~

*A
Collection
of Letters
to
Bereaved
Parents*

~

72

In H. G. Well's haunting story
'The Magic Shop,'
we find a father leading his son
into the shadowy intrigue
of an out-of-the-way magic shop.
The young son holds his father's hand,
reluctant to lose himself
in the mysteries that want to absorb him.

At first the proprietor is not to be found.
Then, as if by magic, he appears
and with the same magic in his
eyes and voice, he entices the young lad to
inquire of the shop on his own.

In wonder the boy reaches out for
this and that.
His confidence increases
until he finally drops his father's hand.
The magic man invites the boy
to see what is in the next room.
The real magic was just beyond the door.
His father is left behind
and out of sight
listening to their voices
becoming more and more distant.

The father's curiosity
turns to caution--turns to fear--
turns to panic.
He calls his son's name; then louder,
and finally it becomes a yell.
He runs into the darkness of the next
room, trips and falls
and lies unconscious.
Coming to,
the father gathers his wits,
finding himself outside on the sidewalk.

The Magic Shop is closed and locked.
The son, calm,
not the least bit concerned,
helps his father to his feet.
The two make their way home.
the young boy
has a parcel of magic tricks
under his arm.

For days the son is mesmerized
by all the packages contain.
One day, the father tells his
son that he tried to find the Magic Shop
to pay for what his son was given.

Oddly enough, he couldn't find
the little shop at all.

The boy said that it was alright.
The Magic Man told him
that some day he would stop by and
. . . collect the bill.

Though this story reads like a bad
dream it soon becomes an index
into exploring all it means
to say goodbye to our children.

The bill of loving your children
is the necessary pain of letting go.
It's what you pay to the magic man.

Our children grow, experience
wonder and imagination.
As High School Graduation Day arrives,
pay careful note of the
expression on many parents' faces--
those quick glances to the floor.
We see smiles tempered with bitten lips
as parents fight to hide the pain,
the bill that is being paid.
The Magic Man is walking quietly across
the gymnasium floor
to collect the bill.

Love comes at a price, the price of grief,
the grief in the pain of letting go,
the grief in the pain of saying,
"goodbye."

A few months later another installment
comes when mom and dad
take Susie to college.

The station wagon is loaded with
the back end touching the pavement
and the front end aimed at Mars.
The dorm room inspected,
the essential "stuff" is unloaded
A final hug. "We'll see you . . ."
the easiest way we know to say goodbye.
All this is followed by the long ride home.
Mom and dad each have their own
window,
their silence, their own space,
to cope with the grief,
the grief, the bill you pay to the
Magic Man,
to love your children
and set them free.

Sometimes, however, the Magic Man
does not come expectantly
at the end of the month.
Sometimes he comes in the middle of the
night--in the guise of a policeman
nervously rapping on the door,
or a doctor grasping a clipboard,
trying to find words
for what went wrong,
or a simple telephone ring.

Sometimes the Magic Man comes
demanding more than grief.
Sometimes he forecloses on our feelings
forcing us into emotional bankruptcy.
Sometimes the grief
demands as much life from those
who mourn as those who die.
I have seen it.
I have seen the Magic Man
come as a thief.
I have walked with parents pondering
a spot in the road where it happened,
absorbing the rage,
the whys, the guilt.
I have stood before graves
witnessing desperate words spoken
to ears that cannot hear.

I have seen the dark side of the
Magic Man.
his wrath, his random vengeance.

In the end, each situation

demands its own dance,
its own music of healing, and letting go.
There are no easy,
universal answers
for those who let go
of their children for good.
Still, of this it can be said,
the Magic Man, who sometimes
demands life for life,
can never take from us
what our child gave us of their love,
nor ever deny what life they
drew out of us,
the capacity to care,
to wonder,
to laugh,
to need another human being,
that we would never have found in
ourselves if the child had not lived.

To hurt so much,
is to have lived so much.

For all the Magic Man demands of us,
he can never demand
our willingness to try again,
to reach our and be vulnerable again.
To live again,
that is the greatest tribute and
fulfillment to all we must leave behind.

With the birth of each relationship,
and with its eventual goodbye,
we are confronted with the fact
that we must pay,
and sometimes dearly,
for the love and wonder
we find and nourish in this world.

We must pay the bill of grief.

We can, it seems,
either find that as reason
to run and hide from life,
afraid of being burnt again,
or we may come to terms with the
Magic Man long before we see him,
determined that his cost,
however dear,
will always be a bargain
and no payment will ever be final.

CONNIE KORDA IS A PARENT BEREAVEMENT COUNSELOR AT THE MAINE MEDICAL CENTER. THIS GENTLE BOOK WAS HER IDEA.

Dear Parents,

Whenever a bereaved parent reaches out to another grieving parent by sharing experiences and pain, a bonding can take place that is mutually healing. When bonding between parents happens, differences that might have kept them from drawing together under ordinary circumstances are transcended and they become one in their understanding.

DEAR
PARENTS
~
A
Collection
of Letters
to
Bereaved
Parents
~
74

I felt it was important to help Joy and Marv gather together letters for this book because these letters have the potential for bonding bereaved parents with one another, thereby softening pain and quieting the frantic search for answers.

As you have read, and in some cases re-read, these letters, we hope you feel a new closeness, a new tenderness, and a strong bonding with all of us.

Connie

If you like, this page can hold your letter —
to other parents, yourself, or your child.

DEAR
PARENTS
~
A
Collection
of Letters
to
Bereaved
Parents
~
76

- Dr Norman Hagley
  Comfort Us Lord, Our Baby Died

- LYNNE BENNETTE BLACKBURN
  Timothy Duck, for children who have a friend die
  I Know I Made It Happen, explains feelings to children
  The Class In Room 44, when a classmate dies

- SAUNI WOOD
  Mamma Mockingbird, the story of Mama Mockingbird's search for her song

- Susan Evans
  Later Courntney, A Mother Says Goodbye

- Linda Leith Musser
  Remember Lee, A Mother's Journey Through Loss

- Kelly Osmont
  More Than Surviving, taking care of yourself while you grieve
  What Can I Say, a guide to helping those who are grieving

- Adina Wrobleski
  Suicide of a Child

- Martha Wegner-Hay
  Embracing Laura, the grief and healing following the death of an infant twin

- Marion Cohen
  She Was Born, She Died, a book of poetry

- Darcie Sims
  Why Are the Casseroles Always Tuna
  If I Could Just See Hope

- Sherokee Ilse
  Empty Arms, for infant loss
  Planning A Precious Goodbye

- Marilyn Gryte
  No New Baby, for brothers and sisters whose sibling dies

- Allie Sims
  Am I Still A Sister

Please write for a free catalog of available resources.